BLACKBELT IN BLACKJACK

PLAYING 21 AS A MARTIAL ART

REVISED AND EXPANDED

BY ARNOLD SNYDER

Blackbelt in Blackjack:
Playing 21 as a Martial Art
Revised and Expanded

Published by: RGE Publishing
414 Santa Clara Avenue
Oakland CA 94610
(510) 465-6452
FAX: (510) 652-4330
Web site: www.rge21.com
E-mail: books@rge21.com

Cover design by Marion Oldenburg

First Edition
1 2 3 4 5 6 7 8 9 10

ISBN 0-910575-05-3

FOR JESSE AND CHELISE

ACKNOWLEDGMENTS

I would like to thank:

Nick Alexander
John Auston
Julian Braun
George C.
Clarke Cant
Sam Case
Moe Cash
Anthony Curtis
Bob Fisher
Steve Forte
Al Francesco
Peter Griffin
John Gwynn
Tommy Hyland
John Imming
John Leib
Max Rubin
Don Schlesinger
G.K. Schroeder
Howard Schwartz
Ralph Stricker
Ed Thorp
Chuck Weinstock
Brother William
Allan Wilson
Stanford Wong
Bill Zender

For valuable contributions. — *A.S.*

CONTENTS

Introduction to the 1998 Edition

What's 1998 to the rest of the world is 36 A.T. (after Thorp) to card counters. It is remarkable that 36 years after Ed Thorp's *Beat the Dealer* (Random House, 1962) was published, the game of casino blackjack offers greater profit opportunities to intelligent players than at any time in the history of the game. Few would have predicted this back then, when the only state in the union where you could legally play casino blackjack was Nevada, and blackjack wasn't even that popular a game (a distant second to craps).

Since the publication of *Beat the Dealer,* virtually hundreds of books on card counting have been published. Dozens of newsletters and periodicals — devoted exclusively to casino blackjack — have come and gone. Blackjack systems are hawked on late night TV infomercials, through audio and video training courses, high priced seminars, and even in adult education classes in community colleges. There are dozens of home computer software programs on the market, for practicing, simulating, analyzing and devising blackjack strategies. Anyone with a PC can now reproduce in a matter of minutes what Ed Thorp once spent months computing on an IBM mainframe. Every casino in the world now provides special training on card counters' tactics for their pit and security personnel. Specialty software is also in use in casino surveillance departments for identifying players who are suspected of utilizing card counting strategies.

Ed Thorp didn't just write a book in 1962; he transformed an industry and altered the consciousness of millions of casino players throughout the world.

This revised and expanded edition of *Blackbelt in Blackjack* has not been rewritten from scratch because I still agree with much of the original 1983 text and recommendations. It is more an expansion of that text than it is a revision of it. The games and the opportunities have changed in the past 15 years, as have my understanding and perspective on the games available.

One major change in the blackjack scene in the past 15 years is that the casinos are now utilizing high-tech surveillance techniques to identify professional players. Computer analysis of betting and playing strategies — both real-time and post-play from video footage — has made it more difficult for big money card counters to fool the casino counter catchers using traditional count strategies with the tried and true parlay betting camouflage techniques. Because whole tables of players are now computer analyzed simultaneously, even low to moderate stakes card counters, who may have been ignored in the past, find themselves being identified and barred.

It used to be a great camouflage technique to always play at tables where bigger action than yours was on the felt. Your relatively small bets rendered you invisible to the pit. Many blackjack experts, myself included, advised: "Never be the biggest bettor at your table." In some casinos, this is no longer such great advice. Nowadays, if any player at your table is betting black ($100+) action, you may be more liable to be caught in the high-tech surveillance net. Of course, if that high roller happens to be a partying fool who has already been rated as a certified idiot by the pit, this table could be a great opportunity. But these days, the danger of detection is increased substantially, because so much of the surveillance is done invisibly, via video cameras. You don't always see the scowling pit boss anymore.

In some parts of the country, card counters can still get away with murder at the tables. Even in Nevada, you'll find vast differences in casino attitudes and policies. Card counters can no longer play strictly according to charts and schedules. You've got to learn to judge games not only by the rules and the number of decks in play, but by what you can get away with, how perceptive they are, how closely they're watching you. Serious players must join the blackjack underground, subscribe to the players' trade publications, surf the Internet BJ message boards for tips and inside information.

So, in this new edition of *Blackbelt,* I will concentrate on some of the advanced strategies that the pros are using to get away with big action — notably, shuffle tracking and team play (or *tracking* and *teaming*). As the casino industry continues to advance technologically, these types of strategies become more important for all card counters, not just high stakes players.

My approach to these strategies will be similar to the approach I have always taken with blackjack strategies. There is strength in simplicity. It is more profitable to make a few strong strategic plays with accuracy than it is to attempt to squeeze every last penny of profit out of the game with complex, brain-straining methods.

I am very pleased to see that the 1983 edition of this book, along with my first two now out-of-print titles — *The Blackjack Formula* (1980) and *Blackjack For Profit* (1981) — have left a mark. When I embarked on this writing career as a self-professed blackjack expert, I knew my ideas faced an uphill battle. To propose the heresy that a highly simplified set of some two dozen playing strategy indices would realize most of the potential profits from card counting, or that an unbalanced counting system, utilizing only half a dozen playing strategy changes, by *running count,* could be considered a "professional-level" system, was contrary to the thinking of the time. I also emphasized that table conditions, and especially deck penetration, far surpassed the system of choice as far as potential profits from card counting. This was a radical idea in the early 1980s.

Today, thanks to the work of numerous other authors and experts since the publication of the 1983 edition of this book, these concepts and approaches to the game have been further examined and refined, and are no longer even considered controversial. Quite frankly, I initially learned about the value of deck penetration from computer simulation results Peter Griffin had published in a technical paper back in 1975. By the early 1980s, none of the major blackjack authors — Ken Uston, Lawrence Revere, Stanford Wong, Julian Braun, Lance Humble — nor any of the lesser authors at that time, including Jerry Patterson, Richard Canfield, John Archer, Stanley Roberts, and others, had yet picked up on the immense effect of deck penetration; or if they had, they totally ignored this factor in their books. Today, no serious book on card counting would ignore the importance of the shuffle point. And most blackjack authorities today would acknowledge that there is little to gain from using more than a few dozen strategy indices, and even that unbalanced running count systems can be played at a professional level.

This edition of *Blackbelt*, as the first book to describe and recommend advanced shuffle-tracking techniques, will likely also raise a ruckus. I suspect my revelations about using rounded "lite" indices will lift a few quizzical eyebrows. And the new methods I am proposing for true count adjustments, one of which can even be used accurately with an unbalanced counting system, should get the experts buzzing.

Little is known of the original blackjack systems. In *Beat the Dealer,* Ed Thorp discusses a number of the first system developers who had colorful names like "Greasy John" and "System Smitty." They had privately worked out crude but effective blackjack strategies with which they'd won a livelihood from the Las Vegas blackjack tables. Until the early sixties and the publication of Dr. Thorp's book, however, most casinos felt that blackjack systems were like all other gambling systems, a lot of bunk. Prior to Thorp, the only card counting system that was recognized by the casinos as valid was "casing the aces," in which a player would markedly increase his bet (like from $5 to $500) in the second half of the deck if no aces had been dealt in the first half. Crude as this counting technique was, it was effective and the casinos knew it. Unfortunately, it was extremely easy for the casinos to detect. Because it was such a weak card counting method, and because the players who used it rarely employed even an approximation of accurate basic strategy, the huge betting spread was necessary for the system to gain an advantage over the house.

In 1956, a group of mathematicians — Roger Baldwin, Wilbert Cantey, Herbert Maisel, and James McDermott — tediously applied the methods of statistical analysis to the game of blackjack and developed a basic strategy which they published in a technical journal for mathematicians. This strategy, if followed rigorously, would narrow the house edge, making blackjack close to a break even proposition for the player over the long run. Though a colloquial version of this paper was later published as a book, *Playing Blackjack to Win* (Barrows & Co., NY, 1957), few gamblers took notice. Gamblers wanted winning systems, not "break even" systems.

One person who took particular note of this technical paper was Dr. Edward O. Thorp, a mathematician. He saw that this strategy had been devised using old-fashioned mechanical adding machines. He had access to what, in the early sixties, was a sophisticated computer. He wrote a more precise program than had been used, and subsequently developed a more accurate strategy. Baldwin, Cantey, Maisel, and McDermott had suggested in their 1957 book that winning strategies might be developed by keeping track of the cards played, and they even proposed their "partial-casing" system which advised strategy changes dependent on whether the last few cards dealt were ten-valued or "low cards." It was five years, however, until Ed Thorp picked up the ball and ran with it.

Blackjack is a difficult game to analyze mathematically because the depletion of the deck, as cards are played, constantly alters the makeup of the remaining deck, thus altering the probabilities of making a hand or busting, wining or losing. It occurred to Dr. Thorp that, using a computer, he could analyze just how the makeup of the deck affected the possible outcomes of the various hands. His method was unique. He wrote a program to analyze the player's best strategy and long run expectation, assuming various cards in turn had been removed from the deck. He noted that the player's chance of winning was dramatically increased when fives were removed from the deck. In fact, to remove any of the "low" cards — 2s, 3s, 4s, 5s, 6s or 7s — was advantageous to the player in varying degrees. On the other hand, if tens or aces were removed, the player's chances were hurt quite dramatically.

Thorp's first winning strategy was based on counting fives. He recommended betting heavily when they were depleted, and also playing a slightly different strategy when no fives were in the deck. His next system — and this is the system upon which all professional level card counting systems in use today are based — was called the "ten-count." In this system, tens and non-tens were counted separately. Larger bets were placed as the proportion of tens to non-tens in the deck became larger.

The ten-count system, as Thorp created it, was not easy to learn nor to apply in a casino. It required keeping two separate backward counts, and computing the ratio of tens to non-tens prior to betting and strategy decisions. Thorp played his system with what today would be considered a wild betting strategy, sometimes jumping from a table-minimum bet of a dollar to a table-maximum of $500. Casinos were unaware of the power of Thorp's system, since his big bets did not identify him as an ace-caser. When they saw some of the "unusual" plays he made — like splitting 8s vs. dealer upcards of tens and aces — many continued dealing their single-deck, hand-held games down to the last card. Players capable of using Thorp's system accurately had an enormous advantage over the house. Players who were capable of following even a crude approximation of Thorp's strategy could win big if they used even a moderate betting spread in the deeply dealt single-deck games that predominated.

Once the Las Vegas casinos realized a legitimate winning system was being employed at their blackjack tables, they took drastic action. They changed the rules of the game. This was in 1964, two years after the original publication of Thorp's *Beat The Dealer.*

The rule changes did not last long because, to the casinos' dismay, players abandoned the blackjack tables rather than play against the new rules. The casinos that changed their rules began losing the enormous blackjack profits that, ironically, had been generated by the publication of Thorp's book. Bracing themselves for the worst, they reverted back to the original rules.

The worst never came. In fact, the opposite occurred. Blackjack became the most popular table game in U.S. casinos. Everyone, it seemed, believed they could beat the game, but few put in the time and effort to learn a legitimate system. Many blackjack systems were sold which were not mathematically valid. Many players who did have valid systems had no understanding of normal fluctuation. They overbet their limited bankrolls and tapped out before they ever had a chance to see the long run profits. Most importantly, casinos learned to recognize card counters by their playing styles.

Card counters jumped their bets suddenly. They paid inordinate attention to everybody's cards. They were quiet. They concentrated. They didn't drink or socialize. They were often young collegiate types who didn't fit in with the normal run of tourists and vacationing businessmen.

Once spotted, a suspected card counter would be silently observed by the pit boss. Surveillance was called. If suspicions were confirmed by the eye-in-the-sky, the dealer would be signaled to shuffle-up on the counter. If the suspect changed tables, the "heat" would follow him. If he did not leave the casino, he would be asked to leave the blackjack tables, and ultimately ordered to leave the casino. Thus, the casinos weeded out the few competent players and let the hoards of fools who thought they could beat the tables with sloppy play and invalid systems play to their heart's content.

A small number of card counters have been able to continue to profit from the game of blackjack. Two factors contribute to the success of the present day counter. First of all, he knows the basic math of the game. He has studied the game and various valid systems and has a realistic attitude about his long and short run expectations. Secondly, he knows the basic psychology of the casino environment. He understands how casinos detect counters and so disguises his play. He is an actor. If he senses heat, he leaves, perhaps to return at a different time when different casino personnel are running the show. He doesn't take chances. There are lots of casinos.

Although three-and-a-half decades have passed since the first valid card counting systems were published, many casinos still offer beatable blackjack games. The math of card counting is easier today than ever. The systems presented in this book are among the easiest-to-learn professional level systems ever devised. This does not mean that you can learn to beat the game of blackjack in an hour. If you are serious about playing blackjack for profit, you should plan to spend quite a bit of time at study and practice to develop your proficiency. I will say this, however: any person with average math ability could learn to count cards at a professional level.

The difficulty of making money as a card counter is not math, but psychology. Some people are good actors. Some are not. Some are very perceptive of others' attitudes and are capable of manipulating people. Some cannot do this. To make it as a card counter, you must often be sociable and friendly to dealers and pit bosses while simultaneously deceiving them into thinking you're just another dumb gambler. Most card counters who experience any long term success thrive on this exhilarating espionage-like aspect of the game. You must be part rogue and part charlatan. You must be cool under pressure. You must have enough money behind you to weather losing streaks without financial worry. You must thrill to beating the casinos at their own game. If you're not in it for the fun as much as for the money, you'll never make it as a counter. Card counting is boring, once mastered. It's a lot of work. Few who try card counting stick with it. It's like most games — chess, tennis, even the stock market; many people "know how to play," but only a few become masters.

This book is titled *Blackbelt in Blackjack: Playing 21 as a Martial Art.* Many of the same talents, skills, and virtues which would earn you a top ranking position in any of the martial arts could also be applied to casino blackjack. The concept of card counting is based on balance, and making your attack when you are in a stronger position. You never make yourself vulnerable to your opponent (the casino), but through your superior knowledge of your opponent's weaknesses (rules, conditions, cards remaining to be played, etc.), you allow your opponent to bring about his own loss. Your strategy is based on simplicity, not complexity. You take no foolish chances. What moves you make are made with precision, with force ($), and perfect timing. Your opponent thinks he can beat you, thinks he is beating you, and does not see the strength of your superior position. You make your moves with a natural ease. Your camouflage, which allows you to win, is your ability to appear as if you are not even trying.

I realize that most of the readers of this book will not go on to become masters of blackjack strategy. With this in mind, I will offer many simplified, albeit less powerful, methods that the casual player may use to better his chances of winning at the blackjack tables. I will also attempt to provide clear explanations of the more powerful techniques so that the casual player will at least understand how and why the advanced systems work. By understanding these concepts, a beginning player who has not developed the skill to apply them will, hopefully, realize his limited abilities, and will not entertain false visions of himself as an unbeatable player.

One thing you must remember: Casinos don't give money away. You have to take it. And contrary to appearances, casinos are holding on to their money with both fists. You've got to be slick to take on the casinos for high stakes, and walk away with your shirt.

1

THE GREAT BLACKJACK HOAX:
An Irreverent Overview of Card Counting

Forty years ago, the number one casino table game in this country, in terms of gross revenues for the casinos, was craps. This was not surprising. Craps was an all American pastime during World War II. After the war, the state of Nevada provided a way for old war buddies to get together and shoot dice through the years.

Today, thanks to Ed Thorp, casinos make their money from blackjack players. They make a lot of money from card counters. Authors and systems sellers make a lot of money from blackjack players who are, or want to be, card counters. Card counting is big business, but the people who make the most money from it are not the card counters. The greatest profit from card counting goes to the casinos. Systems sellers come in a distant second as far as blackjack profits go. Card counters, as a group, are suffering a steadily increasing loss from their blackjack investments of time and money.

A Card Counter Is Born

I am a card counter. I got hooked on blackjack twenty years ago to the point of obsession. I love this game. There is nothing as exciting as beating a casino and walking out the door with more money in your pockets than when you entered. Card counting offers a legitimate thrill. To enter a casino with the ability to beat the house, knowing the casino will be doing everything it can to identify and eliminate such a threat, gives a James-Bond-Spy-vs.-Spy flavor to the experience. The heart races. The feeling is not unlike that which I recall from my childhood when all the kids in my neighborhood would choose up sides for "cops and robbers." I'd forgotten how much fun it was to hide, sneak, run, hold your breath in anticipation . . . Adults don't play that way, except for maybe a few real cops and robbers.

Then I discovered card counting. It took me a year of weekend trips to Nevada, some dozen books on card counting, and another half-dozen books on mathematics, to learn that I didn't have enough money to play the game professionally. Prior to the 1980s, many blackjack authors seemed to neglect the risk factor, or to provide much guidance on bet sizing according to bankroll. The counter's edge is small. The fluctuation of capital is very great. If you do not have a lot of money, you will not last.

I'll never forget my first trip to Nevada as a card counter. I was driving a car that was 15 years old and over-the-hill. It not only guzzled gas but leaked oil. Winding up through the Sierra Nevada Mountains on my way to Lake Tahoe and the casinos of Stateline, I had to stop twice to add a quart of oil and give my overheated wreck a rest. I was with a friend, and we were splitting the cost of the trip. The way we figured it, after paying for gas, oil, motel room and meals, we'd have about $55 left over to play at the $1 blackjack tables.

When I pulled over to the shoulder of the road for my second oil stop, I said to my friend, "It's hard to believe that we're on our way to becoming wealthy. I hope my car makes it up this damn mountain."

"A year from now," my friend responded, "you'll look back on this day and laugh. This is just the beginning."

One year and some dozen trips to Nevada later, I thought back to that first trip and I laughed. I was again on my way to Stateline, this time alone. My car had long since broken down, beyond repair, and I didn't have the money for another car. I was traveling by bus, and the way I figured it, if I was ahead by twenty-five bucks the first day, I could get a motel room and stay for another day. Otherwise, it was back to the Greyhound station that night. About that time I started to realize I'd been deluding myself into believing I'd get rich at this card game.

WHY BLACKJACK IS SO POPULAR

Blackjack has become the casinos' number one moneymaking table game precisely because people believe the game can be beaten. Casinos are forever bemoaning their losses to card counters. They are constantly changing their rules and dealing procedures to make their games tougher for these feared blackjack experts. Casino floormen, with increasing frequency, unceremoniously bar suspected counters from their tables. Projecting this image of counter paranoia is one of the most successful advertising campaigns ever developed. Not one person in a thousand has what it takes to make any significant amount of money playing blackjack, but hundreds of thousands of people have given it a try. Card counting is not difficult for the dedicated practitioner, but few people are dedicated enough, and, as most players discover the hard way, there is more to being a successful card counter than the ability to count cards.

In cynical moments, I see the American public being taken for a ride by the curiously combined forces of the casino industry and the blackjack systems sellers. A tremendous effort is being made to convince people that card counters can get rich quick at the casino blackjack tables.

Many of the biggest and most prestigious publishing houses list books on card counting in their catalogues. Card counting practice programs are available for home computers, as well as in video format. Blackjack "schools" and seminars are churning out thousands of "graduates" per year. Tuitions often run as high as $1,000.

I don't mean to imply that all blackjack system sellers are trying to bilk the public. I am a system seller. I'm the author of nine books on casino blackjack, numerous technical papers, and a quarterly journal for professional and aspiring professional counters. I've written operating manuals for two home computer blackjack programs, and articles on card counting for numerous periodicals. I've acted as informal consultant for a number of high stakes international counting teams. I know the game can be beaten. I know many part-time card counters who regularly beat the tables for significant amounts of money. I know a few players who have made a fortune playing blackjack. But these successful pros are few and far between. Their dedication to the game is beyond that of the average counter. They live and breathe blackjack. They devour every written word on the subject. They drill and practice until they are counting cards in their sleep. They view professional blackjack as a dog-eat-dog business, which it is.

Some blackjack system authors have been honest about their negative experiences at the blackjack tables. Most publishers, however, do not advertise this aspect of the game, nor does the media in general pay it much heed. It's not newsworthy to say, "gambler loses money." Advertisements for blackjack systems promise everything from instant wealth to private airplanes and islands.

The average player has no way of knowing that the author of his system disagrees with the publisher's advertising claims, and sometimes with large portions of the ghostwritten text. The most respected names in the field of blackjack literature have been abused by their publishers, promoters and imitators.

Compound all of this misinformation about card counting with the dozens of books on the market which teach totally inaccurate count strategies, "money management" systems, systems so weak as to be a complete waste of time or too difficult for human players to master, and you can begin to fathom why card counting is the best thing that ever happened to the casino industry in this century.

THE GREAT BLACKJACK MYTH

In New Jersey, in 1982, representing himself before the state supreme court, the late Ken Uston, renowned author of numerous books on card counting, won a landmark case against the casinos. Today, the 14 Atlantic City casinos may no longer bar skillful players from their tables. The immediate response of the casinos to this law was to stop dealing a game that card counters could beat. This is, and always has been, a very easy thing for the casinos to do. Converting their 6-deck shoes to 8-deck shoes, the dealers were simply instructed to deal out only four decks between shuffles. *Voilà!* Card counting became a waste of time!

Within a few months, however, the A.C. casinos threw in the towel and reverted to their prior practice of cutting off only two decks. In an unofficial boycott reminiscent of what happened in Nevada 18 years earlier when some Las Vegas casinos tried to change the rules of the game to thwart Thorp's followers, the players again forced the casinos to loosen up or lose it all.

Never forget that blackjack exists as a beatable game only because the casinos choose to allow it to exist this way. They do not need mechanical shuffle machines, or electronic card readers, or any other high-tech contraptions, to eliminate the potential profits that card counters might extract from the tables. A simple change of rules or dealing procedures could make all of the blackjack games in the world unbeatable by any card counting system, no matter how advanced, in an instant. But, the casinos simply cannot afford to let this happen.

To this day, however, the 8-deck shoes still predominate in Atlantic City, on some of the most difficult to beat blackjack games in the world. Many Nevada casinos, as well as casinos in some 20 other states and around the globe, currently offer blackjack games which are unprofitable for card counters primarily due to the large betting spread which would be necessary to get a small edge. In most cases, casinos protect their games from counters with poor deck penetration. The casinos, naturally, want players to believe that every unbeatable sucker trap, just because it is called "blackjack," is still a game of skill. It is common knowledge among casino executives that hopeful but incompetent and self-deluded card counters, like other gambling "system players," are a major source of income. If card counters actually stopped playing blackjack in the lousy Atlantic City games, the casinos' blackjack profits would nose-dive.

The American public believes blackjack can be beaten, unaware of the effects of many of the game procedures. The casinos continue to bemoan their losses to counters, as if every other person at their tables were getting rich.

What many people — including most card counters, system sellers, dealers, pit bosses, and the media at large — fail to comprehend, is that to be a successful professional card counter takes no less ability, study, dedication, time, and luck, than any other profession, be it real estate, advertising, or fashion photography. Card counting is attempting to inconspicuously, legally, and consistently, siphon large sums of money from a multi-billion dollar industry that is utilizing the most advanced surveillance techniques this side of the Pentagon.

Most card counters believe in the Great Blackjack Myth that flatly states: *A card counter can beat the game of casino blackjack.* The truth is that some card counting strategies can beat some blackjack games, depending on the number of decks being shuffled together, the number of players at the table, the number of cards being dealt out prior to reshuffling, the rule variations, the betting spread being employed, the size of the counter's bankroll, the actual skill of the player at applying the system, etc. In casinos outside of New Jersey, the threat of being barred causes many counters to kill their own chances of winning. In Atlantic City, despite the no-barring law, card counters must still hide their skill because the casinos may enforce other betting restrictions on suspected counters, which eliminate the potential profits from counting cards. So, counters seek out more crowded, less conspicuous tables. They hold down their betting spreads. They make occasional "dumb" playing decisions. All of these camouflage tactics cut into, and often kill, the counter's potential small edge.

Card counters, as a subculture, have developed a unique jargon. One term that all counters understand is "heat." Heat is a pit boss sweating your action, a dealer shuffling the cards any time you raise your bet, or, worst of all, a floorman reading you your rights: *"You may play any of the casino games except blackjack; if you attempt to place a bet at any blackjack table, you may be arrested for trespassing."*

Many counters think they're getting away with murder when they don't get heat from casinos. The truth is that the casinos are swarming with counters, and most counters are easily detectable. By standing behind crowded blackjack tables, and counting down the cards as they are dealt, I can spot many obvious card counters in the course of a few hours. If I can spot them so easily, you can be sure the casino counter catchers can spot them. Most counters follow obvious betting schemes. To be sure, most counters are likely to get heat at one point or another in their playing careers, especially if they don't camouflage their play. But most of the time counters are not bothered by casino personnel. If the casinos actually gave heat to all the card counters at their tables, they would lose hundreds of good (losing) customers every busy night.

I'm not trying to give the impression that dealers and pit bosses are talented con artists who can act like they are afraid of card counters while knowing most counters are losers. Lower level casino employees, such as dealers and pit bosses, know very little about card counting. Even those few who are trained to count cards, in order to recognize counters, often believe that all card counters pose a real threat to their profits. There is no reason for the upper management of the casinos to educate dealers and pit bosses about the realities of card counting. Dealers and pit bosses, like many in the gambling subculture, are often highly superstitious, and ignorant of the mathematics of any of the casinos' games. Casino executives do not discourage unwarranted fears, superstitions, or ignorance in their floor personnel. Counters love to share stories about superstitious pit bosses. To most counters, casino management is "dumb." This reminds me of Lenny Bruce's "Religions, Inc." bit where the fire-and-brimstone preacher is accused of being dumb. "Yeah, I'm a big dummy," he responds to his detractors. "I've got two Lincoln Continentals, that's how damn dumb I am!"

THE FUTURE OF BLACKJACK

So, where is this all going? Are the days numbered for card counters? Many players fear this may be so, especially when you consider all the technological countermeasures that have been developed in the past decade.

Automatic shuffling machines are being introduced on more and more tables. These devices make shuffle tracking impossible, and they make it less time-consuming, therefore less costly, for the dealers to shuffle more frequently. The new continuous auto-shufflers make card counting itself impossible. Various types of "auto-peek" devices are now extensively employed to read the dealers' hole-cards, eliminating the possibilities of most legal hole-card strategies — tell play, warp play, first-basing.

Surveillance software which analyzes the skill levels of blackjack players is now used in many major casinos. Counters who have been capable of fooling the pit bosses for years suddenly find themselves being pulled up by a computer. Prototypes of "smart" blackjack tables — equipped with shoes that can read the cards as they are dealt, keep track of the players' hands and strategies, and record the players' betting histories via magnetized chips — are now being introduced in Nevada.

Even more ominous than these technological horrors are the legal problems card counters face. In Nevada, the Gaming Control Board is supposed to be an agency which protects the rights of both the casinos and the players, ensuring the fairness of the games. To the consternation of blackjack players, this official state agency has officially taken the position that Nevada's cheating statute, which prohibits the casinos from altering the table games in a way that would change the frequency of the payouts, does not apply to blackjack. Because of this ruling, many Nevada casinos now train their dealers in hand-held games to count cards and shuffle up any time the game favors the players, only dealing when the cards favor the house.

In New Jersey, the state supreme court has ruled that players whose civil rights have been violated by the casinos — even if those players are cheated at the tables — may not sue the casinos for damages. They must settle their differences with the Casino Control Commission, a state agency which claims no authority to order monetary reparations to casino patrons.

Card counters must accept the fact that the state gaming regulatory agencies are often corrupt. These "protective" agencies are in fact puppets of the casinos, controlled by the immense wealth of that industry. Because of this, one of the most rewarding aspects of card counting is knowing that you are often taking money from some truly evil entities. The dealers, pit bosses, shift managers, hosts, and most of the individuals a card counter will actually come into contact with in the casinos, are not themselves corrupt. They are worker ants, in the same way that people who work on the assembly line at a cigarette factory, or a munitions plant, are just people who have found a job to do, and they try to do it well, in order to pay the rent and raise their families.

But lurking in the shadows of this gambling business are some truly slimy bastards. This is a nasty business. If you get into card counting with any serious amount of money, you will learn firsthand what a nasty business this is. Though it has been shown over and over in the courts that card counting is 100% legal, nothing more than using your brain to play your hands, card counters are viewed within the industry as parasites, cheats, and enemies to be eliminated by whatever means necessary.

Casinos throughout the world keep "mug books" of card counters' names and photographs, and these photos are hawked and sold on the open market. Despite the fact that these blacklists might violate various consumer laws, the Fair Credit Reporting Act, civil rights, laws against liable, slander, and the invasion of privacy, the state courts and police agencies throughout the U.S. and around the world systematically use these mug books to harass card counters and deny them access to the gaming tables.

The mega-corporations which have taken over the casino industry have a lot of money and a lot of political power. Professional gamblers, on the other hand, are nobodies. Lawmakers know which side their bread is buttered on. The majority of the American public is ignorant of the issues. The small handful of professional players who see their civil rights being trampled, are like a small voice in the wilderness.

When Bill Bible, the Chairman of the Nevada Gaming Control Board, was appointed by President Clinton to the new Federal Commission on Gaming in 1997, the American press reported extensively on the opposition to this appointment by the religious right. The debate centered on the pro-gambling vs. anti-gambling issues, with Bible portrayed by the right wing as the penultimate pro-gambling apologist. Ironically, all the professional gamblers I knew — certainly a pro-gambling lot! — were more vehemently opposed to Bible's appointment than the anti-gambling lobby, as he is held by many gamblers to be personally responsible for the Nevada casinos' right to violate the state's cheating statutes at blackjack.

So, is this 35-year war with the casinos almost over? Is this the beginning of the end?

Hardly. Despite the technology, the politics, the legal persecution, and the immense financial strength of the casino industry, I remain optimistic. With legal blackjack games now being offered in more than 20 states, there are more profit opportunities for card counters today than at any time in the history of card counting. Despite 3+ decades of stupid, sometimes illegal, and often very costly countermeasures, the casinos are not so stupid as to give up all their profits from their biggest moneymaking table game. I fully expect, 15 years from now, that I will be working on another expansion of this text.

BLACKJACK AS A SPORT

People enjoy taking risks. Gambling, of any type, is a rush. Casino blackjack combines this run for the money with a competitive angle, a game of wit and subterfuge. Every turn of the cards is a cliffhanger. Blackjack has become popular, not because people think they can get rich playing it, but because it has been shown to be a game of skill. Card counting is more interesting than picking a number on a roulette wheel, more challenging than pulling the handle of a slot machine. Many people who play blackjack have little interest in any of the other casino games. Most do not seriously dream of getting rich at the blackjack tables. Like myself, they are often people who had never entered a casino until they'd discovered that one of the games could be beaten by applying an intelligent, systematic strategy. It's unfortunate that so many systems sellers, authors and publishers believe that people must be promised great wealth to interest them in casino blackjack.

You don't have to make a hundred thousand dollars to make this game exciting. If you practice hard and you are dedicated, you'll come out ahead of the game in the long run. Why risk your life savings? For most people, the reward is in the play, not the pay. I like to compare card counting to the oriental martial arts. The immediate analogy which comes to mind is between the Aikido master, who may be smaller and less powerful than his opponent, and the card counter, who likewise appears to be the underdog. Yet the master of Aikido conquers his seemingly more powerful opponent through superb balance, exploiting his opponent's weaknesses, and keeping one step ahead of the fight at all times. In essence, this is how a card counter makes money at the blackjack tables.

Eighteen years ago, I realized that the fastest way to make the most money from card counting would be to open my own casino. Unfortunately, my $300 savings was not sufficient seed capital for this venture. I did the next best thing — I started selling inside information about card counting to other players. I set up a network of professional players, mathematicians, and computer experts to share facts, experiences, and research, and started publishing a quarterly technical journal. Yet, I never stopped playing the game for fun, mostly for nickel ($5) chips. In the past few years, my connections with professional blackjack teams and big money players have enabled me to play a lot more at higher stakes, but the game has remained a game for me, in which the challenge means more than the money.

I wouldn't advise any neophyte blackjack enthusiast to quit work and hock his car in order to stake his million-dollar fantasy. If, as you practice basic strategy, you feel the urge to dream about piloting your own airplane to your private island in the Caribbean, think of these reveries in the same way that thousands of chess players imagine going head-to-head with Boris Spasky, or the way a tennis player might fantasize a match with Pete Sampras. The fact that only a handful of tennis players will ever be professional tennis players does not keep millions of amateurs from playing tennis with true passion.

If you have a passion for blackjack, and you apply yourself diligently, the game will likely pay you dividends in both money and enjoyment. There are, to be sure, a handful of blackjack legends who have made a fortune from the tables, and there are many more unknowns who have done the same, steadily, quietly, unsung. I suspect a few readers of this book may ultimately join those professional players. I know a few readers of the last edition of this book turned pro. For all I know, you may be among the pros by the time the next edition of this book comes rolls off the press.

My major joy from this game, however, will continue to come from discovering, analyzing, and revealing its secrets. Over the next fifteen years, I expect to see shuffle-tracking strategies expounded upon by other authors. I feel sure that rounded "lite" strategy tables will gain popularity. I expect to see more running count systems with accurate "Kelly" betting strategies, and further variations on my simplified methods of true count adjustments.

I also expect the casino industry to continue moaning and crying, as a small handful of players get smarter, the games get tougher, surveillance gets more high-tech, and the majority of card counters keep losing their shirts, due to their own sloppy play and general incompetence.

The information which follows is the information you need *today* to keep a few steps ahead of the casinos. Study it. Learn it. And give 'em hell.

2

HOW TO PLAY CASINO BLACKJACK

Before you attempt to learn any winning strategy, it's important that you familiarize yourself with the game of blackjack, as played in a casino, including all rules, procedures, and options.

Blackjack is one of the easiest casino games to play. After an hour of practice with a deck of cards, following the procedures in this chapter, you will find that you can comfortably play blackjack in any casino. You cannot beat the game this easily, but the rules and procedures are simple enough that anyone could understand and play the game with this small amount of practice.

THE TABLE

This is how a casino blackjack tables appears from the top:

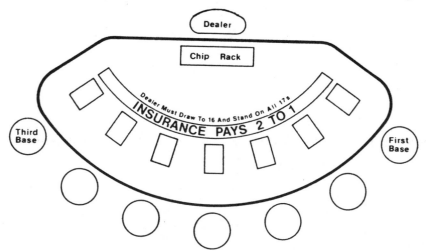

The large circles represent the seats, which can accommodate from one to seven players. The small rectangles represent the marked areas on the table top where players place their bets. There is usually a "limit" sign posted on the table, which states the minimum and maximum bets allowed. Table minimums may run from $1 to $100, and maximums may run from $25 to $10,000. $5 minimum tables are most common. Some states, such as Colorado, have $5 maximums. Some casinos, but not all, also post the rule variations for their games on the table.

The Deal

The cards are dealt from the dealer's left to right, thus the designation of the first seat on the dealer's left as "first base." The last seat is referred to as "third base."

Blackjack was originally dealt from a single 52-card deck of standard playing cards. Many casinos now shuffle together anywhere from one to eight decks. If more than two decks are used, the shuffled cards are placed into a specially designed box on the table called a "shoe," which facilitates the dealing.

The object of the game is to get a total of 21, or as close to it as possible, without going over 21 (busting), and beating the total of the dealer's hand. Players do not play against each other, but only against the dealer, who follows house rules in playing his hand. If a player and dealer tie, it is called a *push,* and neither wins. If the player busts, he loses even if the dealer busts.

In totaling the hands, cards valued 2, 3, 4, 5, 6, 7, 8 and 9 count exactly at their face value, i.e., a deuce counts 2. Cards valued 10, Jack, Queen and King each count 10 points. The ace may count as either 1 or 11, whichever the player prefers.

It makes no difference whether a card is a spade, a heart, a diamond, or a club. Any two-card hand which consists of one ace and on ten-valued card is called a blackjack or a *natural,* and is an automatic win, paid off at the rate of $3 to every $2 bet, or 1½ to 1.

"Hard" Hands and "Soft" Hands

Definition: Any hand in which the ace can be counted as 11, without busting, is a soft hand. Example: You hold an ace and a 7. This is a soft 18. Another example: You hold an ace, a 9, and an 8. This is a hard 18. In this case, if you counted the ace as 11, your total would be 28, a bust. It's important that you be able to read your hand's total value, hard or soft, quickly and effortlessly. When you begin to learn winning strategies, you'll find that hard and soft hands require different decisions. (A hand with no aces is always considered a hard hand.)

THE PLAY OF THE HANDS

The dealer shuffles the deck or decks, then offers the shuffled cards to be cut by a player. Sometimes, in hand-held games, this cut is done exactly as in any home card game. The cards are set on the table by the dealer, and a player simply cuts a portion of the cards from the top of the deck onto the table. In all shoe games, however, and in most hand-held games, a "cut card" is used. This is a specially colored card which a player inserts into the deck to indicate the cut point, where the dealer then completes the cut.

After the cut, the dealer *burns* a card, and sometimes multiple cards. This means that he removes the top card(s) to the bottom of the deck in a single-deck game, or into the "discard tray" in a shoe game.

Before any cards are dealt, all bets must be placed. Each player has a betting spot on the table on which his wager is made. The dealer then deals two cards to each player. The players' cards may be dealt face up or face down. In hand-held games, face-down is more common. In shoe games, face-up is more typical. Since players do not play against each other, but only against the dealer, and since the dealer must play his hand according to preset house rules regardless of what any player holds, it makes no difference if the players' hands are dealt face up or face down. If the players' cards are dealt face up, players are not allowed to touch their cards. If dealt face down, each player must pick up his two cards in order to see his hand and make his playing decisions.

INSURANCE

In most U.S. casinos, *insurance* is allowed. Prior to playing any hands, if the dealer's upcard is an ace, he will ask: "Insurance?" To understand this option, you must know that if the dealer's first two cards are an ace and a ten-valued card, a blackjack, he will automatically beat every player hand on the table except for a player blackjack, which would push his hand. So, when the dealer shows an ace upcard, the player hands are in danger. By offering insurance, the dealer is offering the players a side-bet that he has a natural, i.e., a ten-valued card in the hole. Note the specially marked area on the table layout for insurance bets. If the player is willing to bet that the dealer does, in fact, have a ten-valued card in the hole, for a blackjack, the player places an amount of money equal to up to one-half his original bet in the insurance space. Thus, if a player has $10 bet on the hand, he may make an insurance bet of up to $5, but no more.

After all insurance bets are placed, the dealer peeks at his hole card. If he has a natural, he immediately turns it up and proceeds to pay off insurance bets, and to collect all original wagers placed by the players. Since insurance bets are paid at the rate of 2 to 1, a player with a $10 original bet, and a $5 insurance bet, would lose his original $10, since the dealer's natural is an automatic win, but would be paid $10 (2-to-1) for his $5 insurance bet. Thus, the player breaks even.

If a player has a blackjack when the dealer has an ace up, instead of offering insurance, the dealer usually offers *even money* to this player. This means that before the dealer checks his hole card, the player may accept an even money win for his blackjack. Many players do not understand that an offer of even money is *identical* to an offer of insurance when a player has a blackjack.

This is because a player who takes insurance when he has a blackjack, will ultimately be paid even money *whether or not the dealer has a ten in the hole.* Consider: with $10 bet on your blackjack hand, and a $5 insurance bet, if the dealer *does not* have a ten in the hole, then you will lose your $5 insurance bet, but win $15 (1½ to 1) for your $10 blackjack hand. This is a net win of $10, or *even money.*

On the other hand, if the dealer *does* have a ten in the hole, then you will win $10 (2 to 1) on your $5 insurance bet, but push on your $10 blackjack hand, again for a net win of $10 — *even money.* So, if you have a blackjack, an offer of even money is the *same thing* as an offer of insurance.

If the dealer does not have a natural, all insurance bets are immediately collected by the dealer, and the play of the hands resumes, starting with the first base player and working clockwise.

In some casinos, dealers do not check their hole cards or settle insurance bets until after the play of the hands.

HITTING

Assuming the player does not have a natural, which is an automatic win, the player's most common decision is whether to Hit or Stand. Hitting is taking another card. Example: A player holds a 5 and an 8 for a total of 13. He decides to try to get a total closer to 21, so he signals the dealer for a hit. In a face-up game (i.e., a game in which all players' cards are dealt face up, hence, players are not allowed to touch their cards), the player signals for a hit by scratching or tapping the tabletop with his finger. In a face-down game where the player must pick up his first two cards, the player signals for a hit by scratching or tapping on the tabletop with the edge of his cards. The dealer then deals the player another card face-up on the table. The player may not touch this or any subsequent cards dealt to him. Let's say this card is a deuce. The player may now decide to stand (not take any more cards) or hit again. The player may hit as many times as he chooses, so long as his total does not exceed 21.

STANDING

A player signals he wants to stand by either waving his hand sideways, palm down in a face-up game, or, in a face-down game, by sliding his original two cards face-down beneath his wager.

BUSTING

In a face-down game, if a player hits his hand to a total of more than 21, he should immediately lay his original two cards face up on the table. The dealer will collect the player's wager. In a face-up game, the player need do nothing as the dealer will see the bust, sometimes remarking, "too many," as he collects the bet.

DOUBLING DOWN

A player may also elect to double down on his first two cards. This means that the player doubles the size of his bet, and that he receives one and only one hit card. In the face-up game, this is signaled simply by placing an amount of money on the table, beside the original bet, equal to the amount of his original bet. In the face-down game, the player places his original two cards face up on the table behind his bet, then places an amount of money equal to his original bet beside it in his betting spot. A casino may have restrictions on when a player may double down. Some allow doubling down on any two original cards. Some restrict the doubling down option to hard totals of 9, 10 and 11 only, some to 10 and 11 only. There are even a few casinos that allow doubling down on more than two cards, but this rule variation is rare. Many casinos allow players to "double for less" than the original wager, but none allow players to double down for more.

SPLITTING PAIRS

If a player holds two cards of the same value, he may split the pair into two separate hands. For example, let's say you are dealt two 8's. You do not have to play this as a single hand totaling 16. By placing an amount of money equal to your original bet on the table, you may play each 8 as a separate hand. Again, in the face-up game, you do not touch the cards, but simply take this option by putting your money on the table. In the face-down game, you separate each of your cards face-up on the table, and add the bet for the second hand beside one of the cards. When you split aces, most casinos do not allow more than one additional card on each ace. Likewise, most casinos allow non-ace pairs to be resplit up to four hands. If, for instance, you split a pair of 8s, and received another 8 on one of the hands, most casinos would allow you to resplit and play a third hand.

Usually, split aces may not be resplit. If you receive a ten on one of you split aces, this hand counts as 21, but is not a blackjack. You will not be paid 3 to 2. The dealer will complete his hand, and if he totals 21 also, it is a push. Most casinos allow you to split any ten-valued cards. For instance, you may split a Jack and a King. Some casinos, however, require that only identical ten-valued cards, such as two Kings, may be split. As with split aces, if you split tens and draw an ace on one of them, it is not counted as a blackjack.

Unless informed otherwise, assume the standard pair-splitting rules: Any pair may be split. Any pair, except aces, may be resplit. Split aces receive only one card each.

There are also some casinos which allow you to double down after splitting. For instance, you split a pair of 8s, and on one of the hands you are dealt a 3 for a total of 11. Some casinos will allow you to double down on this hand if you so desire.

SURRENDER

In a few casinos, the player may *surrender* his first two cards and lose only half his bet. This means that the hand will not be played out. The dealer will collect the player's cards and exactly one half the amount the player had wagered. The other half of the wager is returned to the player. Surrender is not allowed if the dealer has a natural, in which case the player loses his whole bet. When the Atlantic City casinos first opened in the late 1970s, they did allow players to surrender before the dealer checked for a natural. This rule is called *early surrender*. It is not currently available in Atlantic City, but has occasionally been offered at other casinos. (The original surrender rule is now often referred to as *late surrender*.) Some casinos in Europe and Asia allow early surrender vs. a ten, but not against an ace.

NO HOLE CARD

In some casinos, the dealer does not check his hole card until after all the players complete their hands. In some casinos, the dealer does not even deal his hole card until the players' hands are completed. This means that the dealer may ultimately get a natural and beat the table. If a player had doubled down or split a pair, he would lose only his original bet, if he were playing in any U.S. or Canadian casino. The European no-hole-card rule is different. In most European casinos, if the player doubles down or splits a pair, he will lose all double and/or split bets if the dealer gets a natural.

Multi-Action

Some casinos use special table layouts which allow players to place up to three simultaneous bets. In these *Multi-Action* games, the player will play his hand once, but the dealer will play out his hand three times. He will use the same upcard, but will draw a new hole card, and hit cards if necessary, against each successive player bet. In these games, all other blackjack rules and options remain the same

The Dealer's Hand

The dealer completes his own hand only after all players have competed their hands. The dealer has no options. He is not allowed to double down or split any pair. He is not allowed to surrender. He must hit any hand which totals less than 17 and stand on any hand which totals 17 or more. The only exception to this is that some casinos require the dealer to hit a soft 17 (such as A,6). In these casinos, the dealer stands on hard 17 or over, and soft 18 or over. In no casino does the dealer have any choice about how to play his hand. He must follow house rules. If, for instance, you are playing in a face-up game and the dealer sees that you have stood on a total of 15, when his hand totals 16, he does not automatically win. He must hit his hand when his total is less than 17, and he will only win your bet if he does not bust.

This covers all of the rules of standard casino blackjack. There are some less common rules you may encounter which do not affect the game significantly. A few casinos offer bonuses for certain player hands, such as a holding of three 7s, or 6, 7, 8 of the same suit. Some casinos offer a blackjack variation called "Double Exposure" in which both of the dealer's first two cards are dealt face up, but the dealer wins all ties. This is a relatively rare game, requiring a different strategy from standard blackjack and is not covered in this book. This game is available at only a few Nevada casinos.

A few casinos also offer various "side-bet" options. Over/Under, Royal Match, and Super Sevens, are among the most common. These types of options allow the player to place a separate bet, usually in a specially marked area of the table layout, and do not affect the play of the regular blackjack hand. As these game variations are rare, and of limited value, they will be explained in more detail in Chapter Sixteen, which deals with special rules.

If you have never played blackjack in a casino, then you should spend an hour playing with a friend or just by yourself, until you feel comfortable with the game. If you have a computer, there are many excellent, inexpensive, software programs available which provide realistic blackjack practice games. When practicing, whether on a computer or your kitchen table, don't worry about minor details, such as the precise method of "scratching" for a hit. You'll understand the correct signals within a few minutes of observation in a casinos. If you're not quite sure of some signal or rule variations when you are playing in a casino, the dealer will be happy to explain if you ask. There is no harm in appearing unknowledgeable in a casino. Casinos cater to tourists, and explaining the procedures of the games is a regular part of their job.

3

Basic Strategy

Once you understand how to play blackjack, you can begin to learn how to play without losing money. If you make your decisions by playing your hunches, you will lose in the long run. There is only one correct decision for any given play, and that decision is based strictly on mathematics. Whether or not you should hit or stand, double down or split a pair, depends on what the laws of probability predict to be your expectations for each of these possibilities. Mathematicians, using high speed computers, have analyzed every possible hand you might hold vs. every possible dealer up card.

Definition: Basic strategy is the mathematically optimum way to play your hands if you are not counting cards. Depending on the rules and the number of decks in use, basic strategy will usually cut the house edge to no more than about ½ percent over the player. This makes blackjack the least disadvantageous game in the casino, even if you are not a card counter.

To explain why the various basic strategy decisions are best would require extensive mathematical proof. Unless you understand the math, and have a computer to work it out, you'll have to accept basic strategy on faith. There is an underlying logic to basic strategy, however, which can be understood by anyone who understands the rules of blackjack.

Why Basic Strategy Works

In a 52-card deck there are 16 ten-valued cards: four tens, four jacks, four queens, and four kings. (For purposes of simplification, when I refer to a card as a "ten" or "X," it is understood to mean any 10, Jack, Queen or King.) Every other denomination has only four cards, one of each suit. You are four times more likely to pull a ten out of the deck than, say, a deuce. Because of this, when the dealer's upcard is "high" — 7,8,9,X, or A — he has a greater likelihood of finishing with a strong total than when his upcard is "low" — 2,3,4,5, or 6.

Thus, if the dealer's upcard is a 7, 8, 9, X, or A, and you were holding a "stiff" — any hand totaling 12 through 16 — you would hit. When the dealer's hand indicates strength, you do not want to stand with a weak hand. Even though, when you hit a stiff, you are more likely to bust than to make a pat hand, you will lose more money in the long run if you stand on these weak hands when the dealer shows strength.

On the other hand, if the dealer's up card is 2, 3, 4, 5 or 6, and you were holding a stiff hand, you should stand. Since he must hit his stiff hands, and since stiffs bust more often than not, hitting your weak hand is not advantageous.

Similarly, if the dealer's up card indicates he may be stiff, you would find it more advantageous to double down or to split pairs, thereby getting more money onto the table when the dealer has a high chance of busting. You double down and split pairs less often when the dealer shows a strong upcard.

This is the basic logic of casino blackjack. There are exceptions to these oversimplified guidelines, as the actual basic strategy decision for any given hand is determined by working out all of the mathematical probabilities.

USING THE BASIC STRATEGY CHART

Do not attempt to learn all aspects of basic strategy at once. Regardless of the number of decks in play or the rule variations, basic strategy for any game is essentially the same. Since few casinos offer the late surrender option, you need not learn this unless you intend to play in those casinos. Since the early surrender option is so rare, the basic strategy for this rule variation is primarily of academic interest only. It is not included in these charts. Should you encounter a casino which offers this option, you will find the basic strategy for it in the Appendix.

The basic strategy chart presented here is a "composite" basic strategy, good for any set of rules and any number of decks. Actually, as these conditions change, some of the basic strategy decisions also change. Usually, these changes are for borderline decisions, and do not significantly change your expectation. I know a number of high stakes pros who know only one basic strategy and ignore the fine changes caused by rule variations and the number of decks in play. In the Appendix, a complete basic strategy, including all the changes according to rule and deck variations is presented. This is for advanced players, or for players who expect to do most of their playing under the same set of rules and conditions, and who would like to play accurately. For now, I advise learning this composite basic strategy, which may be all you will ever need.

Two pair-splitting tables are presented here. Note that I use the symbol "$" to denote a basic strategy split decision. The first pair-split table assumes that you are *not* allowed to double down after splitting a pair. In most casinos, this is the rule, though in some casinos, including all Atlantic City casinos, players are allowed to double down after pair splits. If you plan to play primarily in Atlantic City, study the second table. Note that there are only a few differences between these tables. If you'll be playing in games with both rules, just learn the first table, then brush up on the differences prior to playing in the double-after-split (DAS) casinos.

Note that I use the symbol "¢" to denote a basic strategy surrender decision.

The charts on pages 32-33 are straightforward. The player's hands are listed vertically down the left side. The dealer's upcards are listed horizontally along the top. Thus, if you hold a hand totaling 14 vs. a dealer 6, you can see the basic strategy decision is "S", or Stand. With a total of 14 vs. a dealer 7, since "S" is not indicated, you would hit. Note: If your total of 14 is comprised of a pair of 7s, you must consult the pair splitting chart first. You can see that with a pair of 7s vs. either a dealer 6 or 7, you would split your 7s.

ORDER OF DECISIONS

Use the basic strategy chart in this order:

1. If surrender is allowed, this takes priority over any other decision. If basic strategy calls for surrender, throw in the hand.

2. If you have a pair, determine whether or not basic strategy calls for a split.

BASIC STRATEGY
FOR ANY NUMBER OF DECKS

	2	3	4	5	6	7	8	9	X	A
					STAND					
17	S	S	S	S	S	S	S	S	S	S
16	S	S	S	S	S	H	H	H	H	H
15	S	S	S	S	S	H	H	H	H	H
14	S	S	S	S	S	H	H	H	H	H
13	S	S	S	S	S	H	H	H	H	H
12	H	H	S	S	S	H	H	H	H	H
A7	S	S	S	S	S	S	S	H	H	H

DOUBLE DOWN

	2	3	4	5	6	7	8	9	X	A
11	D	D	D	D	D	D	D	D	D	D
10	D	D	D	D	D	D	D	D		
9		D	D	D	D					
A7		D	D	D	D					
A6		D	D	D	D					
A5			D	D	D					
A4			D	D	D					
A3				D	D					
A2				D	D					

SURRENDER (LATE)

	2	3	4	5	6	7	8	9	X	A
16								¢	¢	¢
15									¢	

S = Stand   H = Hit   D = Double Down   ¢ = Surrender

This generic basic strategy may be used for any game. See Appendix for all basic strategy variations according to rules and number of decks in play.

PAIR SPLITS

	2	3	4	5	6	7	8	9	X	A
NO DOUBLE AFTER SPLITS										
AA	$	$	$	$	$	$	$	$	$	$
99	$	$	$	$	$		$	$		
88	$	$	$	$	$	$	$	$	$	$
77	$	$	$	$	$	$				
66		$	$	$	$					
33			$	$	$	$				
22			$	$	$	$				
WITH DOUBLE AFTER SPLITS										
AA	$	$	$	$	$	$	$	$	$	$
99	$	$	$	$	$		$	$		
88	$	$	$	$	$	$	$	$	$	$
77	$	$	$	$	$	$				
66	$	$	$	$	$					
44				$	$					
33	$	$	$	$	$	$				
22	$	$	$	$	$	$				

INSURANCE: NO

$ = Split

3. If you have a possible double down hand, this play takes priority over hitting or standing. For instance, in Las Vegas and Atlantic City, you may double down on any two cards. Thus, with a holding of A,7 (soft 18) vs. a dealer 5, your basic strategy play, as per the chart, is to double down. In Northern Nevada, where you may usually double down on 10 or 11 only, your correct play would be to stand.

4. After determining that you do not want to surrender, split a pair, or double down, consult the "Stand" chart. Always hit a hard total of 11 or below. Always stand on a hard total of 17 or higher. For all "stiff" hands, hard 12 through 16, consult the basic strategy chart. Always hit soft 17 (A,6) or below. Always stand on soft 19 (A,8) or higher. With a soft 18 (A,7), consult the chart.

How to Practice Basic Strategy

1. Study the Charts

Any professional card counter could easily and quickly reproduce from memory a set of basic strategy charts. Study the charts one section at a time. Start with the hard Stand decisions. Look at the chart. Observe the pattern of the decisions as they appear in the chart, close your eyes and visualize this pattern. Study the chart once more, then get out your pencil and paper. Reproduce the hard Stand chart. Do this for each section of the chart separately — hard Stand, soft Stand, hard Double Down, soft Double Down, Pair Splits, and Surrender. Do this until you have mastered the charts.

2. Practice with Cards

Place an ace face up on a table to represent the dealer's up card. Shuffle the rest of the cards, then deal two cards face up to yourself. Do not deal the dealer a down card. Look at your two cards and the dealer's ace and make your basic strategy decision. Check the chart to see if you are correct. Do not complete your hand. If the decision is "hit," don't bother to take the hit card. After you've made and double-checked your decision, deal another two cards to yourself. Don't bother to pick up your first hand. Just drop your next, and all subsequent, cards face up on top of the last cards dealt. Go through the entire deck (25 hands), then change the dealer's up card to a deuce, then to a 3, 4, 5, etc. You should be able to run through a full deck of player hands for all ten dealer up cards in less than half an hour once you are able to make your decisions without consulting the charts. Every decision should be instantaneous when you are proficient. Strive for perfection. If you have the slightest doubt about any decision, consult the chart.

To practice your pair split decisions, which occur less frequently than other decisions, reverse the above exercise. Deal yourself a pair of aces, then run through the deck changing only the dealer's up card. Then give yourself a pair of deuces, etc. Don't waste time with any exercise you don't need. Your basic strategy for splitting aces, for instance, is always to split them. You don't need to run through a whole deck of dealer up cards every day to practice this decision. Likewise, basic strategy tells you to always split 8s, and never to split 4s, 5s or 10s. You will learn these decisions quickly. Most of your study and practice for pair-splitting decisions should go toward learning when to split 2s, 3s, 6s, 7s and 9s.

If you learn to play basic strategy without counting cards, most casinos will have only a ½ percent edge over you. This means that in the long run, they will win about 50¢ for every $100 you bet. In some games, the house advantage over basic strategy players is slightly more or less than this. If you play blackjack for high stakes, it is wise to learn basic strategy, even if you are not inclined to count cards. Playing basic strategy accurately will greatly cut your losses.

SIMPLIFIED BASIC STRATEGY

If you do not intend to learn accurate basic strategy, you can cut the house edge to about 1 percent by playing an approximate basic strategy. Follow these rules:

1. Never take insurance.

2. If the dealer's upcard is 7, 8, 9, X or A, hit until you get to hard 17 or more.

3. If the dealer's upcard is 2, 3, 4, 5 or 6, stand on all your stiffs; hard 12 through 16.

4. Hit all soft hands of soft 17 (A,6) and below.

5. Stand on soft 18 (A,7) or higher.

6. Double down on 10 and 11 vs. any dealer up card from 2 through 9.

7. Always split aces and 8s.

8. Never split 4s, 5s or 10s.

9. Split all other pairs — 2s, 3s, 6s, 7s and 9s — vs. any dealer up card of 4, 5 or 6.

10. Surrender 16 vs. 9, X or A.

Note: In Multi-Action games, your basic strategy does not change. Always play every hand exactly as if it were the only hand on the table. Do not be afraid to hit your stiffs — a common Multi-Action error. The Multi-Action format does not alter the house percentage, or basic strategy, in any way.

If you intend to learn to count cards, first learn to play accurate basic strategy. Once you know basic strategy, your decisions will become automatic. Assuming you brush up on your charts occasionally, you will not have to continue practicing basic strategy. Even when you are counting cards, you will play basic strategy on 80% or more of your hands. *Basic strategy is your single most powerful weapon.*

4

THE RED SEVEN COUNT

BALANCED VS. UNBALANCED COUNTING SYSTEMS

Most professional level card counting systems are *balanced* point count systems. Plus and minus point values are assigned to the various cards, and as these cards are seen, the player adds the point values in his head to his running count. Once learned, this aspect of card counting becomes automatic and easy. The count system is said to be "balanced" because there are an equal number of "plus" and "minus" point values. The sum of all these plus and minus values is zero. The difficulty of playing a balanced point-count system comes when attempting to use the running count for betting and strategy decisions. First, the running count must be converted to a true count (see Chapter Ten for an in-depth explanation of true count). Second, the player must have memorized, and be able to apply, the correct strategy index number for each decision.

Learning to keep a running count is not difficult for most players. Applying the count properly at the tables, however, is such a mental strain that many either give up on card counting completely, or continue to count but extract very little value from their halfhearted efforts.

UNBALANCED SYSTEMS

In 1969, a Berkeley math professor, using the pseudonym "Jacques Noir," wrote a book called *Casino Holiday,* which contained an "unbalanced" ten count system which required no true count conversions. Within a few years, more refined versions of Noir's running count system were published by Stanley Roberts

(1971), then John Archer (1973). The power of the Noir count derives from its built-in imbalance which makes it very simple to play. Tens are counted as -2, and all non-tens, including aces, are counted as +1. We call this an "unbalanced" count because the count values of the complete deck, when added together, do not equal zero. Because of the imbalance, however, no true count adjustments are necessary for many important decisions.

If you count down a deck using this count, any time your running count is +4, then the ratio of non-tens to tens is exactly 2-to-1. Thus, this count is a perfect insurance indicator by running count. This count has one major weakness, and that is in its betting efficiency. The ten count has a betting correlation of only 72 percent. Compare this to Hi-Opt I's 88 percent, or the Hi-Lo count's 97 percent correlation.

Quite a few players still chose to use this unbalanced ten count, despite its betting weakness, because they did not consider their abilities in making true count conversions to be very accurate anyway. Both Roberts and Archer advised players to keep a side-count of aces, which could greatly improve the poor betting efficiency of the Noir count. Because of the added difficulty of keeping a side count, then using it to adjust the primary count, many Noir counters simply ignored the side-count advice.

Why, I asked myself, is this unbalanced ten count, which had been around for more than a decade, the only unbalanced count system ever invented? Why not an unbalanced point count system, which would be optimized to indicate perfect *betting* by running count, rather than perfect insurance?

THE RED SEVEN COUNT

Thus, in 1983, was born the Red Seven Count. When the first edition of this book was published, many blackjack authorities expressed disbelief that such a simple counting system could be so strong. Peter Griffin, whose monumental *Theory of Blackjack* (GBC, 1979) established him as the reigning blackjack math guru — a position he still holds, and deservedly so! — reviewed the first edition of *Blackbelt in Blackjack* in GBC's *Casino & Sports #23* (1983):

> *Arnold Snyder's latest offering will undoubtedly prove to be a mild disappointment . . . I have a developing*

sense that Snyder enjoys being different and provocative. This probably accounts for his advocacy of the "Red Seven" system. . . . Snyder bases his assertion of the dominance of unbalanced counts over balanced counts on the existence of a "pivot." . . .What Snyder appears unaware of is that a balanced count also has a pivot, and that pivot is zero. This locates a far more useful and common point of reference. . .

Given Griffin's stature in the blackjack community, and the fact that I had developed the Red Seven system almost entirely from the data in *Theory of Blackjack,* which was my bible, I was crushed. Within weeks of his review, I was being barraged with letters from those who had already purchased *Blackbelt in Blackjack,* asking me if I had revised my opinion about the strength of the Red Seven, in light of Griffin's review. Many pointed out that Joel Friedman, in that same issue of *Casino & Sports,* also expressed disappointment, pointing out that the Red Seven was weaker than traditional counting systems.

I had claimed in the 1983 *Blackbelt in Blackjack,* that despite its running count simplicity and a playing strategy that advised only half-a-dozen changes from basic strategy according to that count, that the Red Seven system would capture 80 percent of the profit potential of the traditional balanced point count systems in multiple-deck games, even when those systems used 100+ strategy changes, all made perfectly according to the authors' advised true count conversion method.

This was in the pre-PC days of blackjack, when you couldn't just sit down at your home computer and whip out a few million hands to test a system. If you weren't a programmer yourself with access to a million-dollar mainframe through some university or major corporation, simulation testing of blackjack systems was not feasible.

Despite Griffin's reputation, and his nonpareil comprehension of the mathematics of the game, I felt certain that the Red Seven would perform as I claimed, capturing 80 percent of the profit potential of the more difficult true count systems.

So, I enlisted Peter Griffin's colleague at California State University, Dr. John Gwynn, Jr., to test the Red Seven Count via computer simulation. I assured Dr. Gwynn that regardless of the results he obtained, and even if they proved the Red Seven system to be far less powerful than I'd claimed, I would publish his results in *Blackjack Forum* exactly as I received them.

I asked him to simulate the Red Seven Count, exactly as I had published it, with only 6 strategy changes, all made by running count, in two common games (at that time), and to compare the Red Seven results with two versions of the Hi-Lo Count, as published by Stanford Wong in *Professional Blackjack,* one version utilizing all 184 indices by true count, and one using Wong's condensed -6 to +6 version (34 indices) by true count.

I published Gwynn's results in the December 1983 issue of *Blackjack Forum:*

4 Decks, 75% Dealt, Vegas Strip Rules, 1-10 Spread

	# Indices	Win Rate
Red Seven	6	0.77%
Hi-Lo (condensed)	34	0.87%
Hi-Lo (complete)	184	0.87%

1 Deck, 75% Dealt, Reno Rules, 1-3 Spread

	# Indices	Win Rate
Red Seven	6	0.73%
Hi-Lo (condensed)	34	0.89%

John Gwynn did not test the 184-index version of the Hi-Lo in the one-deck game, though it surely would have outperformed the 34-index version, probably by a couple tenths of a percent. He tested the full-blown Hi-Lo in the shoe game because I had also expressed the opinion that card counters were wasting their time memorizing 100+ index numbers for shoe games. I had published my Zen Count system in 1981 with only 25 indices, and had stated that no counting system needed more than these for multiple-deck games. This was another area of great controversy at that time, though today, thanks to Don Schlesinger and others, this simplified approach is embraced by most experts as common wisdom.

Gwynn's computer results, which substantiated my claims of the Red Seven's power, surprised many knowledgeable experts, and revolutionized blackjack system development. Many other authors devised unbalanced point count systems. Ken Uston self-published his "Uston SS Count." Uston, in fact, hired me

BLACKBELT IN BLACKJACK ERRATA

There are two MAJOR errors. Please replace the charts on pages 41 and 44 with the following:

Page 41:

THE RED SEVEN POINT VALUES

Learn to count cards by adding and subtracting the following values as the respective cards are removed from the deck:

Ace:	-1
10:	-1
9:	0
8:	0
Black 7:	0
Red 7:	+1
6:	+1
5:	+1
4:	+1
3:	+1
2:	+1

Page 44:

RED SEVEN STARTING COUNTS

# DECKS	STARTING COUNT
1	-2
2	-4
3	-6
4	-8
5	-10
6	-12
7	-14
8	-16

to produce the strategy charts for him. George C. came out with his "Unbalanced Zen 11." Eddie Olsen, with assistance from Michael Dalton, presented his "TruCount" system. Most recently, Olaf Vancura and Ken Fuchs published their popular "Knock-Out" system.

The Red Seven Point Values

Learn to count cards by adding and subtracting the following values as the respective cards are removed from the deck:

Ace:	**+1**
10:	**-1**
9:	**0**
8:	**0**
Black 7:	**0**
Red 7:	**+1**
6:	**+1**
5:	**+1**
4:	**+1**
3:	**+1**
2:	**+1**

The one strange mechanism here is that I am suggesting that you count black 7s as 0, and red 7s as +1! This is the device which creates the exact imbalance necessary for this count to work as a running count system. (Technically, it does not make any difference whether the red seven or the black seven is counted, so long as this precise imbalance is attained. One may even count all sevens as $+\frac{1}{2}$, or simply count every other seven seen as +1.)

How to Practice Counting

Start by buying yourself a couple dozen decks of cards. Put one in the pocket of every one of your jackets. Put one by each telephone you use regularly. One on the kitchen table. One by each TV set. One on the dashboard of your car. Always have a deck of cards at hand. As you watch TV, talk on the phone, or enjoy your morning coffee, practice keeping your running count using the above point values for the individual cards as you turn them over.

Start your count at 0. Turn cards one at a time face-up onto the bottom of the deck, adding each card's point value to your running count. For example:

Cards seen: 2, A, 8, 9, X, X, 5

Point values: +1, -1, 0, 0, -1, -1, +1

Running Count: +1, 0, 0, 0, -1, -2, -1

By the time you get to the end of the deck, your running count should be +2. If it is not +2, then you have not counted correctly, assuming your deck contains 52 cards. If you have miscounted, turn the deck over and run through the cards again, until your final running count is +2. Then shuffle and go through the deck once more. Build up speed and accuracy.

When you are proficient at counting down a deck of cards in this manner, practice turning the cards over two at a time, and learn to count cards in pairs. It's faster and easier for most people to count cards in pairs. This is because many pairs cancel each other out. For instance, every time you pair a ten or ace (both -1) with a 2, 3, 4, 5, 6, or red 7 (all +1), the pair counts as zero. You will quickly learn to ignore self-canceled pairs, as well as 8s, 9s and black 7s, since all of these are valued at 0. When you are good at counting cards in pairs, start turning them over 3 at a time. You must be accurate in your count. Speed without accuracy is worthless. It may take you weeks to become proficient at keeping a running count, but once you learn it, it's like telling time. You'll find you can do it almost automatically, and with very few errors.

As a self-test after you can count cards in pairs and groups of three, run through the cards by fanning them from one hand to the other as you count. Allow your eyes to quickly scan the exposed cards for self-canceling pairs, even when these cards are not adjacent to each other. You should be able to count down a deck in this fashion in 40 seconds or less before you ever attempt counting in a casino. Most pros can easily count down a deck in less than 30 seconds. Most professional teams require players to demonstrate that they can count down a deck in 25 seconds or less, with perfect accuracy every time.

No matter how fast you get at counting by turning cards over yourself, you'll probably find counting at a casino blackjack table to be difficult initially. In face-down games, some cards will appear as mere flashes as players throw in their hands, and dealers scoop up cards as quickly as they're turned over. Before you try counting cards in a casino, while playing blackjack, spend a half-hour or so counting while watching others play. Do not sit down to play until you feel comfortable counting while watching the game.

If you expect to play in shoe games, practice counting down multiple decks of cards at home. Note that your final count is always 2 times the number of decks you are using. With six decks, your running count at the end should always be +12. With two decks, it would be +4.

THE STARTING COUNT

In the first edition of this book, I advised Red Seven players to always start counting at zero, regardless of the number of decks in play. Using this counting procedure, the player adjusted his "pivot" count by multiplying the number of decks in play by 2. I.e., with six decks, we defined the pivot as +12. In a single-deck game, the pivot was +2. With an unbalanced count, we make most of our playing and betting decisions according to the pivot count.

There is a more practical way to use unbalanced counts for players who are frequently changing games, playing vs. various numbers of decks, and especially if using extended strategy indices. Instead of altering the pivot count according to the number of decks in play, you can alter the *starting count* so that the pivot remains the same. Instead of starting your count at zero off the top of the deck(s), subtract the pivot count from zero, and start counting at a negative number.

In 1986, when Ken Uston hired me to help him devise his unbalanced SS Count, he wanted to provide more complete strategy tables, with separate sets of charts for each number of decks. I had no difficulty devising the charts, but some of the multiple-deck indices were very high numbers. Since Uston's level-three count had an imbalance of +4 per deck, his 8-deck pivot was +32, and his index number for hitting 15 vs. 10 was +44. His 6-deck index for this decision was +33. His 4-deck index for 14 vs. 10

was +40. Even his 2-deck number for this decision was +22. Ken felt these numbers were unwieldy, and I agreed.

The device we decided to use for the SS Count was a "Starting Count" other than zero. Multiplying -4 x the number of decks in play, the SS one-deck starting count became -4; the eight-deck starting count became -32. Thus, the SS pivot was always 0, regardless of the number of decks in play, and the strategy charts look a lot less intimidating. A few years later, when George C. developed an unbalanced version of my Zen Count, he used this same device.

With the Red Seven Count, we'll use this technique for adjusting the starting count, always making the starting count -2 x the number of decks in play. I.e., the 4-deck starting count is: -2 x 4 = -8. This methodology will always make your pivot = 0.

RED SEVEN STARTING COUNTS

# DECKS	STARTING COUNT
1	0
2	-4
3	-6
4	-8
5	-10
6	-12
7	-14
8	-16

Now, when you practice counting, always start at the appropriate starting count for the number of decks you are using. Your pivot is always 0, and when you come to the end of the deck(s), you should always have a final running count of 0.

THE RED SEVEN BETTING STRATEGY

Once you are proficient at counting, you can begin to apply the Red Seven betting strategy at the tables. Remember, when counting in a casino, that you always begin your count at the appropriate starting count for the number of decks in play after each shuffle. Any time your running count is 0, your advantage will have risen about 1 percent over your starting advantage. This zero pivot is a good indicator of when to raise your bet for nearly all the blackjack games available in this country. About 90 percent of the games in this country have a starting advantage between -0.4 percent and -0.6 percent. So, your zero pivot usually indicates an advantage for you of approximately ½ percent. In Chapter Six, you will find a method for determining the house starting advantage more precisely according to the rules and the number of decks in play.

Simply stated, the Red Seven betting strategy is to bet more when your running count is 0 or higher, and less (or nothing) when your running count is negative.

How much of a betting spread should you use? This depends on many factors — the rules of the game, the number of decks in play, the penetration (shuffle point), the size of your bankroll, what you can actually get away with in that particular casino, etc. All of these topics will be covered in depth in the chapters which follow. For now, the chart below will provide a guide for the most common games.

		Units to Bet	
Running Count	**1 Deck**	**2 Decks**	**Shoe**
Negative	1	1	1 (or 0)
0	2	2	2
+2	4	2	2
+4	6	3	2
+6	8	4	3
+8	8	6	4
+12	8	8	6
+16	8	8	8

Note that the suggested bets are in units, not dollars. In the next chapter you will find guidelines on how to size your bets according to your bankroll. The above guidelines are not to be taken as strict betting advice. In many one-deck games, a 1-to-8 spread according to the count will get you booted out in short order. In many shoe games, a 1-to-8 spread would barely get you over the break even point. This is why the 0 unit bet is suggested in shoe games at negative counts. It is often impossible to only play at positive counts in shoe games, but it is often wise to leave the table at negative counts. You will find more advice about this type of tablehopping approach in the following chapter also. The above chart should be used as a general guide for casual players.

Serious players will need to use much more precise betting strategies, according to their advantage, table conditions, the necessity for camouflage, etc.

THE RED SEVEN PLAYING STRATEGY

What about the major playing strategy decisions? Using the Red Seven Count, you can also increase your advantage over the house by deviating from basic strategy according to your running count.

First of all, insurance is the most important strategy decision. In single-deck games, assuming you are using a moderate betting spread, insurance is almost as important as all other strategy decisions combined. Conveniently, you have a very nice insurance indicator with the Red Seven Count. In 1- and 2-deck games, you simply take insurance any time your running count is 0 or higher. In all shoe games, take insurance at +2.

As for other playing decisions, there are only a few to remember. Any time you are at 0 or higher (any number of decks), stand on 16 vs. 10 and on 12 vs. 3. (According to basic strategy, you would hit both of these.) In single-deck games, the 16 vs. 10 decision is the second most important strategy decision for a card counter — insurance being first. After you find these strategy changes easy, there are a couple of others you can add which will increase your advantage a bit more. At running counts of +2 or higher, with any number of decks, stand on 12 vs. 2, and on 15 vs. 10; and double down on 10 vs. X.

In multi-deck games, by using this simple running count strategy, you will be taking advantage of about 80% of all possible gains from card counting. Because you will not be sloppily attempting to adjust your running count to true count on every hand, your decisions will be made with devastating accuracy. Using the simple Red Seven Count, you have no strategy tables to memorize. You simply have a basic strategy, which you play on more than 90% of your hands, and so few changes that you will make according to your running count that it would be pointless to draw up a chart.

There are, to be sure, weaknesses in this vastly simplified system. However, in my opinion, most card counters would be wise to ignore more difficult strategies. Because of its combined power and simplicity, the Red Seven Count lends itself to many advanced professional approaches to beating the game of black-jack. It works excellently for tablehopping (Chapter 10) and "one-deck Wonging" (Chapter 11). It's also an excellent system for teams and partners (Chapter 15). The Red Seven Count requires the minimum amount of memory work for a professional level system, and also relieves the player from all mathematical calculations at the table, except for the simple adding and subtracting necessary to keep the running count.

If you find it very confusing to be adding and subtracting when your running count is negative, you may totally avoid negative running counts by adding 50 to all of the recommended starting counts, which will also make your pivot 50, instead of 0, with any number of decks. For instance, adding 50 to the 1-deck starting count of -2 makes your starting count 48. Since the 6-deck starting count is -12, if you add 50 to it you get a starting count of 38. Your pivot will now always be 50, and the strategy changes that you would normally make at +2 are now made at 52. Again, I advise this only for players who have trouble dealing with negative numbers. If that's you, then go back to the starting count chart on page 44, and pencil in the corrected starting counts. Now use these numbers when you practice counting down decks. There is no loss of power if you use this method.

THE ADVANCED RED SEVEN COUNT

For those players who are bitten hard by the blackjack bug, who might be considering moving on to a more advanced true count system, let me suggest that you first try the Advanced Red Seven. This system uses the same Red Seven count values, and continues to work as a running count system, but we expand on the strategy changes so that you may play more accurately. For dedicated players there is also a precise method of estimating your advantage, so that you may utilize the same proportional betting schemes that professional players use.

HOW TO READ THE STRATEGY CHARTS

In the 1 & 2-Deck Strategy Chart, the **heavy bold** index numbers are to be used for both 1- and 2-deck games. For 2-deck games, these are *all the indices you will use*. The lighter numbers may be used *for single-deck games only*. They are not as impor-

The Advanced Red Seven

1 & 2-Deck Strategy

	2	3	4	5	6	7	8	9	X	A
16							6	**2**	**-2**	4
15							6	4	**2**	4
14	-4	-4							6	
13	-2	-2	-2							
12	**2**	**0**	**0**	**-2**	**-2**					
11								-4	-4	**-2**
10							-4	-2	**2**	**2**
9	**0**					2				

Insurance: **0**

Surrender

	2	3	4	5	6	7	8	9	X	A
15								**2**	**0**	**0**
14									**2**	

BOLD = 1 & 2-Deck   Light = 1-Deck Only

All Shoe Games

	2	3	4	5	6	7	8	9	X	A
16								4	-4	
15									4	4
14										
13										
12	4	0	-4							
11										-4
10									4	4
9	-4					4				

Insurance: 4

Surrender

	2	3	4	5	6	7	8	9	X	A
15								0	-4	0
14									4	

tant as the bold indices, so if you play in single-deck games, the bold indices should be learned first.

The Shoe Game Chart is to be used only in the *second half of the shoe.* I.e., in an 8-deck game, use the Advanced Red Seven indices only after the first four decks are in the discard tray. In a 6-deck game, wait until three decks have been played to start using the advanced indices. In the first half of the shoe, follow the simple Red seven strategy, utilizing only the half-dozen strategy changes listed on page 46.

Note that the shoe game indices are quite different from the 1- and 2-deck indices. If you sometimes play in shoe games, and sometimes in hand-held games, then I would suggest learning the 1- and 2-deck chart for the hand-held games, but when you play in shoe games, revert to the simple Red Seven system, using only the half dozen indices prescribed earlier. Naturally, if you find memory work easy, or if you are very dedicated, you could learn both of these charts. Do not try to do more than you are mentally comfortable with. Remember that it is better to do a few things correctly than to make errors attempting to do too much.

These charts are presented in the standard format of blackjack strategy charts, like the basic strategy charts in Chapter 3. *If there is no entry for a decision, then you should always use basic strategy.* No pair split indices are provided because the gains are too small to bother with. For all of the player hand totals of 12-16 at the top of the charts, the index numbers are the running counts at which you should *stand.* For example, with 12 vs. 4 in the Shoe Game chart, note that you will stand if your running count is -4 or higher. This means that in the second half of the shoe, you would stand on a count of -4, -3, -2, etc., and hit on -5, -6, -7, etc.

If surrender is allowed, surrendering takes precedence over other decisions. Since no indices are provided for surrendering 16 vs. 9, 10, or A, always follow basic strategy and surrender these hands.

The easiest way to learn the index numbers is to learn them in blocks. First learn all of the 0 (pivot) indices. Then learn the +2 indices, then the +4 indices. After you have learned all the positive indices, learn the negative indices, starting with the -2s. Many players make flash cards to drill themselves on index numbers. There are also many excellent software programs available which allow you to input and practice card counting systems.

The Advanced Red Seven "True Edge"

There is a simple and accurate method for estimating your advantage with the Advanced Red Seven Count. I do not recommend this method for any player who finds it confusing or difficult. Such players must resign themselves to using the betting chart on p. 45, along with the advice on bet sizing according to your bankroll in the following chapter.

Advanced players, however, will want to bet more precisely according to their exact advantage over the house. You may do this with the same precision as the balanced true count systems by using your running count to make a simple fraction that equates to your *true edge* over the house.

Many professional players have shied away from the unbalanced counting systems because without a "true count," it is impossible to follow a proportional betting scheme, where each bet is dictated by the approximate advantage on the hand about to be dealt. The true edge method solves that problem, not by first converting the running count to a true count which, can then be used to estimate the advantage, but by directly converting the running count into the precise fractional percent advantage.

Make a Fraction

First of all, any time your running count is negative, assume that either the house has the advantage, or your advantage is less than ½ percent, so you do not want to bet much more than one unit regardless. *Make a fraction only when your running count is positive.*

Every fraction has two parts, a *numerator* and a *denominator*. The numerator is on top, and the denominator is on the bottom:

$$\frac{numerator}{denominator}$$

In the fraction ½, numerator is 1, and the denominator is 2. To estimate your precise advantage with the Red Seven Count, your numerator, the top number, is your current running count. I.e., If your running is +6, the fraction becomes:

6

denominator

The denominator is simply *twice the number of decks remaining to be dealt.* For example, let's say you are in an eight-deck game, and your running count is +6. Two decks have been dealt, with six remaining in the shoe. Your numerator is simply 6 (your running count). Your denominator is 6 (number of decks remaining) x 2 = 12. So your fraction is:

$$\frac{6}{12} = \frac{1}{2}$$

This means your advantage has risen by exactly ½ percent above your pivot advantage. If this were a typical eight-deck Atlantic City game, where your pivot (0) indicated a ½ percent advantage, then this +6 running count with 6 decks remaining means your advantage has gone up another ½ percent, so that you now have a full 1 percent advantage over the house.

Note that in order to estimate your true edge, you simply add the amount of the fraction you make with your running count to your pivot advantage.

Consider what happens to your advantage if, in this same eight-deck game, your running count is +6, but 5 decks have been dealt out, leaving only 3 undealt in the shoe. Your denominator becomes 3 x 2 = 6; and your fraction is:

$$\frac{6}{6} = 1$$

So, at this point in the shoe, your +6 running count indicates a full 1 percent raise in your advantage above your ½ percent pivot advantage, and your total advantage over the house is now 1½ percent.

Another example: assume that in this same game you have a running count of +6, but now six of the eight decks have been dealt, with only two remaining in the shoe. Using the true edge method, your denominator is 2 x 2 = 4, and your fraction is:

$$\frac{6}{4} = 1½$$

This deep in the shoe, your +6 running count indicates a 1½ percent raise above your ½ percent pivot advantage, so that your total advantage over the house is now 2 percent.

Note that as the shoe is dealt deeper, the same +6 running count indicates a raise from your pivot advantage of anywhere from ½ percent to 1½ percent. In fact, if this shoe were dealt very deeply, and you found yourself with a +6 running count with only 1 deck remaining, your advantage will have risen by:

$$\frac{6}{1 \times 2} = \frac{6}{2} = 3\%$$

Technically, we are simply applying standard true count theory in a unique way in order to calculate the actual raise in advantage when the running count rises above the pivot. The advantages we are calculating with this method are 100% as precise as the standard balanced true count methods used by most pros. From the examples above, you can see why professional players have always steered away from the running count systems. If you were to always bet according to your running count, then depending on the level of penetration, you will often be either overbetting or underbetting your true advantage. The true edge method solves this problem.

I have used simple examples above, so that the fractions we came up with were easy. With very little practice, however, you should discover that you have no difficulty estimating your raise in advantage, even when the numbers are not so convenient.

For instance, what if you are in an eight-deck game, with a running count of +4, and 3½ decks are remaining to be dealt. Since 3½ x 2 = 7, your fraction becomes:

$$\frac{4}{7}$$

This may be an unusual fraction, but you should be able to determine in an instant that it's just slightly more than ½ percent. Likewise, with fractions like 5/7 or 6/7, just knowing that your advantage has risen more than ½ percent but less than 1 percent is all you need for purposes of bet sizing.

In using this method, always round *up* to the nearest half-deck when you estimate the remaining decks for your denominator. For instance, if slightly *less than* five decks have been dealt, so that you estimate about 3¼ decks remain, round this *up* to 3½, and your denominator becomes 3½ x 2 = 7. This way, your denominator will always be a *whole number,* which is very convenient. This method also assures that you are being *conservative* in estimating your advantage, and therefore, safer in bet sizing.

If you have any difficulty whatsoever calculating your denominator when ½-deck increments are involved, then simply memorize the following chart:

½	x	2	=	1
1½	x	2	=	3
2½	x	2	=	5
3½	x	2	=	7
4½	x	2	=	9
5½	x	2	=	11
6½	x	2	=	13
7½	x	2	=	15

I think most people of average math abilities can do this with little difficulty, but if you have trouble, then simply learn the chart.

Also, let me reemphasize that you should not be intimidated by "weird" fractions. If you come up with fractions like:

$$\frac{5}{13}, \frac{2}{5}, \frac{5}{11}, \frac{4}{9},$$

so long as you know that these fractions are all less than ½ — or even somewhere around ½ — you have all the information you need to estimate your advantage. Most pros estimate their advantage to the nearest ½ percent. It's impractical to attempt to size your bets with more accuracy than this. Likewise:

$$\frac{12}{10}, \frac{11}{8}, \frac{9}{7}, \text{ and } \frac{5}{4},$$

are all slightly more than 1. Knowing that your advantage has gone up slightly more than 1 percent above your pivot advantage is all you need to know. You do not need to consider 9/7 as anything different from 12/10. For your betting purposes, just consider all of these fractions indicative of a 1 percent raise above your pivot advantage.

If you use the true edge method in single-deck games, in the first half of the deck, you simply divide your running count by 2 (since your denominator is 1 x 2). So, a running count of +3 indicates about a 1½ percent raise from your pivot advantage. +4 would be a 2% raise, etc. At the half-deck level, your raise in advantage *is your running count,* since ½ x 2 = 1, and if you divide any number by 1, the answer is the same number. I.e., with a +5 running count and half a deck dealt, your advantage has risen 5 percent. So, in single-deck games, don't even bother to make a fraction. In the top half of the deck, divide by 2. In the bottom half, just use the running count. Should you ever play in a really deeply dealt one-deck game, in the bottom quarter deck, you can actually multiply your running count by 2! I.e., a +3 count would equal a 6 percent raise in advantage. Low stakes players may occasionally find games like this.

One convenient feature of the Advanced Red Seven Count is that all strategy decisions, which often must be made very quickly, are still made by running count. The betting decisions, for which you always have a few more moments to decide, can be made with all the accuracy of a true count system, simply by using the true edge method of directly converting your running count to your raise in advantage.

A mathematician and longtime correspondent, Conrad Membrino, who has published the derivation of the methodology for true count conversions with unbalanced counts, believes that estimating your true advantage with an unbalanced system would tend to introduce *less error* into the calculated advantage than the traditional true count methods with balanced counting systems. (Interested math nuts will find Membrino's paper on the Blackjack Forum Web Site, at http://www.rge21.com, in the free library section.)

If you use the true edge method of estimating your advantage, you should also employ the same proportional betting techniques that professional players use, based on the "Kelly Criterion." You will want to read the following chapter on bankroll requirements, as well as the chapters that follow on true count, betting strategies, and all other advanced topics, in order to develop the best betting strategies for your bankroll, the games you are attacking, your style of play, etc.

♠ ♣ ♥ ♦

5

HOW MUCH MONEY DO YOU NEED?

Before we go much further in our study of the nuts and bolts of card counting, there is one simple mathematical formula you should learn. I call this formula the Profit Formula. You may use this formula to get a handle on what your expectation from the blackjack tables might be, based on your average bet size.

THE PROFIT FORMULA

Average Bet x Advantage x Hands Per Hour = Hourly Profit

The formula is simple, yet it provides a good approximation of what a card counter might expect to win per hour in the long run. Say you are making average bets of $10 with a 1 percent advantage over the house from card counting. You estimate you're playing about 80 hands per hour. To calculate your expected hourly win:

$10 x .01 x 80 = $8 per hour.

(Note that your 1 percent advantage is expressed decimally as .01, for use in the formula. A 2 percent advantage would be .02, a 1½ percent advantage would be .015, etc. You might find it helpful to follow this math with a pocket calculator.)

Now, let's say you want to increase your expectation above $8 per hour. That's simple enough to do, keeping the Profit Formula in mind. Simply raise the value of one or more of the three vital factors in the formula.

Start with the first factor: *average bet*. Obviously, if you made an average bet of $25, your expectation would immediately rise to $20 per hour:

$$\$25 \times .01 \times 80 = \$20 \text{ per hour.}$$

That's simple, but there is a problem if you have a limited bankroll. Increasing your bet size leads to greater fluctuation. Although your long run win rate may rise to $20 per hour, you may never see the long run. Do you have a sufficient bankroll to increase your average bet size to this level? *Don't guess!* Keep reading. . .

The next variable in the Profit Formula is *advantage.* It's simple enough to see how to raise your expectation to $20 per hour by altering this factor; just raise your advantage to $2\frac{1}{2}$ percent. Thus:

$$\$10 \times .025 \times 80 = \$20 \text{ per hour.}$$

This is the tactic most card counters attempt to employ. They start using an "advanced," higher level, "multi-parameter" system. They keep side counts of aces, and sometimes fives or sevens, and memorize extensive strategy tables.

Unfortunately, this tactic does not pay off as well as most counters would like to think. Even the most advanced system will rarely raise your advantage by more than $\frac{1}{4}$ percent to $\frac{1}{2}$ percent over your advantage with a simple system, such as the Red Seven Count.

If you're playing with black ($100) chips, a $\frac{1}{4}$ percent increase in your win rate may be worth the trouble, if you can play an advanced strategy with speed and accuracy. If not, you may be wasting your time, or even lowering your win rate.

Consider a game which would net the Red Seven Count about 1 percent, and would net a more advanced system about $1\frac{1}{4}$ percent. Whereas, the Red Seven Count would win at a rate of $8 per hour, the advanced system would win at a rate of only about $10 per hour if you can play it with equal speed and accuracy.

$$\$10 \times .0125 \times 80 = \$10 \text{ per hour.}$$

So, if it's $20 per hour you're shooting for, this tactic won't accomplish your goal. By all means, go for the greater win if you can do it. But don't delude yourself if you find yourself struggling with decisions at the table. You're mental efforts are unlikely to pay of in dollars and cents.

For the average card counter, there is little to gain from an advanced counting strategy. Most players would either slow down so much, or play so inaccurately, that they would gain nothing. Many would actually decrease their win rates.

The last factor in the Profit Formula is *hands per hour*. Most blackjack authors estimate that a player gets about 75 to 100 hands per hour. Full tables may cut this down to 60 hands per hour, or even fewer if other players at the table are slow. Head-on play, when you can find it, will get you about 200 hands per hour.

Many players do not believe they can find head-on games, and when they can, they do not believe they can play 200 hands per hour. Actually, this is a pretty normal rate of play in a head-on game — if you do not waste time making your decisions.

Playing faster is more challenging, and is also an excellent cover. Dealers and pit bosses expect card counters to play slowly and thoughtfully. In hand-held games, dealers will sometimes deal deeper into the deck for fast players, which is a further advantage (see Chapter Six). After all, the faster you play, the more often the dealer must shuffle. If you're accomplished enough as a counter to carry on some semblance of small talk while playing your hands at a good clip, you will likely be judged as no threat to the house.

To find head-on games (also often called heads-up, or head-to-head), especially at low stakes, you must play at off hours. Mornings and early afternoons on weekdays are excellent times to go hunting for dealers who are standing behind empty tables twiddling their thumbs. There are, to be sure, other arguments — pro and con — with regards to playing under various crowd conditions for purposes of camouflage, team/partner attacks, etc. I will attempt to cover all of these considerations later. For now, it's important that you understand the basic math of how a card counter estimates his win rate in dollars and cents.

In a game where 80 hands per hour nets you $10 per hour, 200 hands per hour will raise your expectation to:

$$\$10 \times .01 \times 200 = \$20 \text{ per hour.}$$

And this assumes the same average bet size, and the same percent advantage from your card counting efforts. One question that many neophyte counters ask is: *How much money can I make?* The answer, as you can see, is not so cut and dried. *Every one of the factors in the Profit Formula is a variable, and every one has a big effect on the answer.*

System sellers who make claims that using their blackjack system will net you $XXX per day, per week, or per year, are generally peddling baloney. Unless they fill in all the variables of the Profit Formula — which will differ for every player, and change according to the table conditions you face — any such claim is pure speculation.

To optimally apply the Red Seven Count, or any other card counting system, you'll need to learn much more about such factors as table conditions, betting strategies, camouflage, toking, and every other aspect of casino blackjack that is important to a professional player.

But how do you figure out your average bet size? You don't just pick a number out of thin air and decide to bet that much per hand. Any pro will tell you that the most important factor in bet sizing is the size of your playing bankroll.

ALLOWING FOR NORMAL FLUCTUATION

So, before we go any further into the techniques of card counting, let's look at some of the practical considerations of bankrolling your play. Essentially, what you are up against is what mathematicians call *normal fluctuation.*

When you count cards, sometimes you will win, and sometimes you will lose. In the short run, anything can happen. This is true even for the casinos. Although the casinos enjoy a large edge on their slot machines, some slot players on some days win more than they lose. This is why people return to the slots. If all slot players lost every time they played, no one would play.

Let's stick with blackjack, though. Assume you learn to play basic strategy, so that you nearly eliminate the house edge. How much can you win or lose due to normal fluctuation?

Start by considering all of your bets to be of equal size. Rather than assigning some $ value, let's say you are betting one unit on each hand. We will assume you are in a single-deck Las Vegas Strip game, playing perfect basic strategy, so that for all intents and purposes, the game is dead even. Over the long run, you'd expect to win nothing and lose nothing. It's like flipping a coin.

Of course, if you try flipping a coin a thousand times, and recording the results, you'd be highly unlikely to come up with exactly 500 wins and 500 losses. There are precise mathematical formulas for predicting the limits of normal fluctuation. With an introductory course in probability and statistics, you would know how to make such estimations. For now, let's develop some practical guidelines describing the best and worst you might expect due to normal fluctuation.

Statisticians use the term *standard deviation* to explain variations from the expected result. For instance, if you flip an honest coin 10 times, your expected result is five heads and five tails. If, however, you came up with 7 heads and 3 tails, this would not be indicative that the coin was dishonest. It would be considered a normal fluctuation. However, if you flipped a coin ten thousand times, and it came up 7,000 heads and only 3,000 tails, it would be very unlikely that this were an honest coin. Even though the ratio of heads to tails has remained 7 to 3, the large number of tosses make the result highly unlikely.

Standard deviation is a function of the square root of the number of trials. It is not difficult to figure out on any pocket calculator that has a square root key. The square root of 100 is 10, because 10 x 10 = 100. The square root of 1,000 is approximately 31.6 because 31.6 x 31.6 = 1,000, approximately.

When you understand what the square root of a number means to a statistician, you will understand why it is perfectly normal for you to come up with 7 heads out of 10 flips of a coin, but nearly impossible for you to come up with 7,000 out of 10,000 flips, assuming the coin is honest.

The square root of 10 = 3.16. To a statistician, 3.16 is one standard deviation.

The square root of 10,000 = 100. So, 100 is one standard deviation on 10,000 trials.

So, to come up with 7 heads out of ten flips, is to be 2 heads away from our expectation of 5. We are well within one standard deviation (3.16).

But to come up with 7,000 heads out of 10,000 flips, is to be 2,000 heads over our expectation of 5,000. And since one standard deviation on 10,000 flips is only 100, this result is 20 standard deviations away from our expectation. Statistically, this is nearly impossible.

How impossible is it?

Statistically, we expect to be within one standard deviation 68 percent of the time. We will be within two standard deviations of our expectation 95 percent of the time. We will be within three standard deviations 99.7 percent of the time. Suffice it to say that if we get a coin flip result that is 20 standard deviations from our expectation, either the coin or the flipper are crooked. You have a better chance of winning your state lottery than you do of flipping these 7,000 heads.

All blackjack players must be concerned with normal fluctuations, as you must size your bets according to both your advantage and the size of your bankroll. I will provide guidelines based upon statistical realities that should be sufficient for most casual players. Serious players will find excellent references in the Appendix for further study.

In an hour of play, or about one hundred hands, in a dead even game, you will not usually be ahead or behind by more than 20 units. On rare occasions, however, in a single hour of play, you may expect to be ahead or behind as many as 35-40 units.

If you play off and on over a period of a few days — say, ten hours of play, or about a thousand hands — you will not usually be ahead or behind by more than 75 units. On rare occasions, you might be ahead or behind by 120 units in a one-thousand-hand period. These estimates of fluctuation assume you are always betting only one unit on each hand, and that neither you nor the house has any significant long run advantage.

Your Bankroll

So, how big should your playing bankroll be? *Definition: Bankroll — the amount of money you can afford to lose, over a specified period of time.* Ask yourself, "How much can I afford to lose this weekend, painlessly?" That is the size of your bankroll for this weekend. How big of a unit can you afford to play with? Divide your weekend bankroll by 120. That is your safe betting unit. If you intend to play longer than one weekend, and especially if you are serious about card counting for profit, you must use more sophisticated methods of bet-sizing. But let's stick with the basics for now. Even if you do not go on to become a serious card counter, you should understand the basics of normal fluctuation if you ever gamble in casino games, even for fun.

When you first start to play blackjack in a casino environment, regardless of whether you are playing basic strategy only or attempting to count cards, your first sessions must be viewed as practice sessions. There a number of betting guidelines you can follow when initially practicing in casinos, which will prepare you for the more difficult techniques of bet-sizing when you are counting cards and playing seriously. These guidelines do not comprise a winning system, but are merely a practice exercise which will train you to size your bets in proportion to your bankroll. Later, when you are counting cards, you will use these same techniques in conjunction with other methods.

Your bankroll, in units, must be able to withstand the short run fluctuations. If you have a total of about $500 "play money," you would be courting disaster if you started making $25 bets. $500 would represent only 20 units of $25 each, and you could easily lose your whole stake in less than an hour. Making $10 bets would be safer, since you would have 50 units to play with, but this could also be lost in a relatively short run of hands just due to fluctuation. With $5 bets, or 100 units, you'd be unlikely to lose your whole bankroll in a single weekend of play, though even this would be possible.

The first step to proportional bet-sizing is to constantly reassess the size of your bankroll and, based on this reassessment, to systematically change the size of your betting unit. Here's how to do it:

Bet-Sizing for a Weekend (1,000) Hands

First, divide your total bankroll into one hundred units. Let's assume you have $1000, so you have one hundred $10 units. This is your bet size. Here's how to handle a losing streak:

If you lose twenty units, or $200, quit play and reassess your bankroll. Since you now have only $800, you divide this into one hundred units, and your new unit becomes $8. Play at this level until your bankroll either fluctuates back up to $1,000, or continues to spiral downward to $600. Whichever way the fluctuations go, continue to reassess the size of your bankroll, and resize your bets accordingly, so that you never bet much more than 1 percent of your total bankroll on any given hand.

None of this will have any effect on the fact that over the long run, your expectation will be to break even, assuming you're playing in an even game. In a slightly negative expectation game, the house will slowly grind you down the longer you play. The purpose of the above betting method is primarily to train you to constantly monitor your bankroll size, and to keep you in the game longer when you hit a losing streak. It will not give you any long run advantage. In fact, if you are not playing with an advantage, as we assume here, you may expect that on some weekend, or series of weekends, you may lose your entire $1,000 bankroll just due to normal fluctuations. This is especially true if you must practice in casinos where the table minimums are $5, so that you cannot reduce your bet any more if your bankroll dips below $500.

If you are practicing in a casino where you must place $5 minimum bets, and your starting bankroll is $1000, you would be wise to start out with a $5 betting unit and never vary from this, unless you came ahead a few hundred dollars.

If your starting bankroll is less than $1000, or if $1000 represents a significant amount of money to you, play only table minimum bets when practicing. Be aware that you must view this money as "play money," as you could conceivably lose it all due to normal fluctuation.

If the house has a slight edge ($\frac{1}{2}$ percent is typical), you may still use the above guidelines for sizing your bets. Be aware that when the house has an edge, your bankroll will *inevitably* be depleted over the long run. In the short run, anything can happen.

For card counters, and especially for high stakes card counters, bet-sizing is more complex than the simple guidelines presented here. We will get into bet-sizing for advanced players in Chapter Ten of this book, since these techniques will not concern you until you have acquired considerable skill and experience.

The betting guidelines in this chapter are presented for beginners to use when practicing at low stakes. If you have a $50,000 bankroll, you would be ill-advised to follow the guidelines in this chapter, i.e., divide this bankroll into 100 units of $500 each, in a break-even (or negative-edge) game, just so you could practice basic strategy. Why chance losing 20 to 30 thousand dollars in a short period of play just for practice? Practice at low stakes, then use your big money to bankroll your play when you know what you're doing.

If you have a personal computer, then by all means acquire one of the excellent software programs on the market that allow you to practice blackjack systems. Save your casino practice until you are an accomplished card counter. Practicing in a casino will always be more expensive than practicing at home. Get your basic skills down with as little expense as possible.

Bet-Sizing for a Month (10,000 Hands)

Let's say you are planning an extended session of playing blackjack during a 3- or 4-week trip, and you expect to play for a total of about 100 hours, or about 10,000 hands. After playing this many hands, you would not usually be ahead or behind by more than 250 units, but on rare occasions, you might find yourself ahead or behind by as many as 400 units, due to normal fluctuation.

For this reasons, if your total playing bankroll is only a few thousand dollars or less, you could conceivably lose it all, due to normal fluctuation, even if you become an expert card counter. You could ultimately be a victim of the table minimum bets. If, as your losing streak continued, you were allowed to cut back to bets of $3, then $2, $1, etc., you would probably never lose all of your money. In the long run, your losing streak would end, and your edge over the house would begin to pay off. But casinos do set minimum betting requirements. If your bankroll is insufficient, you should not be making any bets at all.

Most players, of course, will not immediately experience inordinate losing streaks, and some will even experience inordinate winning streaks. Fluctuation is probably the leading deterrent to card counting. Most beginning counters overbet their bankrolls. Those with negative fluctuations give up. Those with positive fluctuations usually increase the size of their bets proportionately, thus continuing to overbet their bankrolls, until their first big negative swing wipes them out.

Bet-sizing for a 3- or 4-week period of play (10,000 hands), works exactly the same as bet-sizing for a weekend. The only difference is that you should start by dividing your bankroll by 250, instead of 100, in order to determine your betting unit. In other words, to make $10 bets, you should have a bankroll of $2,500. Cut back to an $8 betting unit if your bankroll goes down to $2,000; $6 units if it falls to $1,500, etc.

As you can see, the greater the number of hands you will be playing, the larger your bankroll must be to ensure your continuance in the game — even when the game is a break even proposition. In fact, the only way to get around this is to get the edge in your favor. If you can get the edge in your favor, via card counting, then in the long run, your edge will assure you that your expected winnings will be greater than the possible negative fluctuations (assuming you also have the fortitude to continue hammering away at the tables through all the ups and downs).

To last in this game, you must have sufficient money. You must size your bets in proportion to your bankroll. You must reassess your bankroll frequently. You must never chase losses by increasing your bet size to win back the money you've lost. If you follow these guidelines, you will have staying power at the tables. If you persevere and acquire skill as a counter, you're on your way to winning.

6

TABLE CONDITIONS

Many card counters believe that as long as a game is called "blackjack," and is being offered by a legitimate casino, they can win by applying their counting systems. The fact is: some games can be beaten by some card counting strategies, but many cannot. Table conditions make the difference. I've written two books on this subject already, my first two books: *The Blackjack Formula* (RGE, 1980), and *Blackjack for Profit* (RGE, 1981). Both books are now out of print. In this chapter, I will attempt to update and condense some of the most important information from these books so that you may choose your games wisely. There are simple guidelines you can follow which will help to keep you from throwing your money away in unbeatable games.

First, let's define table conditions. There are four distinct conditions of any blackjack game which directly affect the profit potential for card counters:

1. *Number of decks in play.* In U.S. casinos, this may currently range from one to eight.

2. *Rules.* There are about twenty common rule variations, and dozens of uncommon variations, in U.S. casinos.

3. *Crowd conditions.* You may be the only player at the table, or one of as many as seven.

4. *Depth of deal,* or *deck penetration,* between shuffles. Anywhere from 20% to 90% of the cards may be dealt out.

Let's go through these conditions one at a time.

1. THE NUMBER OF DECKS IN PLAY

First consider the effect of the number of decks shuffled together. All other conditions being equal, single-deck games would be the most profitable for card counters. The more decks being used, the less profitable the game becomes, not only for counters, but for basic strategy players as well. A single-deck Vegas Strip game (see p. 67), for instance, is pretty close to being a break even proposition for a basic strategy player. With four or more decks in play, and the same set of rules, the house has about a ½ percent edge. Use this chart to estimate your basic strategy (dis)advantage due to the number of decks in play:

# Decks	Advantage
1	+0.02%
2	-0.31%
3	-0.43%
4	-0.48%
5	-0.52%
6	-0.54%
7	-0.55%
8	-0.57%

2. THE RULES

The second condition you must consider is the set of rules used on the game. Some rules, notably those which offer the player more options, are favorable to the player, assuming the player applies the correct strategy. Such rules would be surrender, doubling after splitting allowed, resplitting aces allowed, etc. Those rules which limit the player's options, such as doubling down on 10-11 only, or no resplits, are disadvantageous to the player.

Some rules neither limit nor offer options to the player, but alter the dealer's procedure. An example of one such rule would be "dealer hits soft seventeen." This is disadvantageous to the player. An advantageous dealer rule, used occasionally in short-term special promotions, would be "blackjack pays 2-to-1."

A different type of advantageous rules for the player are the "bonus" rules, such as "dealer pays $XXX bonus to player hand of 6, 7, 8 same suit." Most bonuses have very small value to the player.

In Chapter Two, most of the common rules were explained. In this chapter, we'll look at the approximate effect of each rule on your basic strategy expectation. By adding the effect of the number of decks in play to the effects of the rule variations, you will know the house advantage against basic strategy players. Card counters call this the *starting advantage,* or the advantage *off the top.*

Most rules, to be sure, affect card counters differently than they affect basic strategy players. The house edge off the top, however, is always an important consideration, as this is what your skillful play must overcome. For instance, insurance has no value to a basic strategy player, since correct basic strategy is to never take insurance. If a casino disallows insurance, however, this hurts card counters, since counters profit from their selective insurance bets. Likewise, the surrender option has little value to basic strategy players, less than one-tenth of 1 percent increase in expectation. For a card counter, however, surrender is, like insurance, very valuable.

In order to figure out our starting advantage, we need to begin by defining a benchmark game, i.e., a set of standard rules to which we can add or subtract the effects of the rule variations. Most authors define this benchmark game as Vegas Strip rules:

1. Dealer stands on soft 17.
2. You may double down on any 2 original cards.
3. You may not double down after splitting a pair.
4. You may split any pair.
5. You may resplit any pair except aces.
6. Split aces receive only one card each.
7. No surrender.
8. Dealer either receives a hole card, or the player's original bet only is lost if the player doubles down or splits a pair and the dealer gets a blackjack.
9. Insurance is allowed up to one-half the player's bet, and pays 2 to 1.
10. Player blackjack is paid 3 to 2.

The effect of any other rules must be accounted for in determining your starting advantage. These are the rule effects:

Rule	Effects in Percent		
	1-Deck	**2-Deck**	**Multi-Deck**
Double on 10-11 only:	-0.26	-0.21	-0.18
Double on 9-10-11 only:	-0.13	-0.11	-0.09
Hits Soft 17:	-0.19	-0.20	-0.21
No Resplits:	-0.02	-0.03	-0.04
No Hole Card (European):	-0.10	-0.11	-0.11
Double After Splits:	+0.14	+0.14	+0.14
Double 3 or More Cards:	+0.24	+0.24	+0.24
Resplit Aces:	+0.03	+0.05	+0.07
Draw to Split Aces:	+0.14	+0.14	+0.14
Surrender:	+0.02	+0.05	+0.08
Early Surrender:	+0.62	+0.62	+0.63
Early Surrender (hit soft 17):	+0.70	+0.71	+0.72
Early Surrender v. 10 only:	+0.19	+0.21	+0.24
2-to-1 BJ payoff:	+2.32	+2.28	+2.26
No Insurance:	0.00	0.00	0.00
Multi-Action:	0.00	0.00	0.00
Over/Under:	0.00	0.00	0.00
Royal Match	0.00	0.00	0.00

Most of these rule effects have been calculated by using data from Peter Griffin's *Theory of Blackjack*. Note that the last four rules show effects of 0.00 percent for basic strategy players.

I did not include any of the typical "bonus" rules in this list. The most common of these are 6,7,8 suited or 7,7,7, will pay some bonus amount to the player. The value of such bonuses is generally small. The general rule is to never change your basic strategy to attempt to get a bonus payout. In many cases, the value in percent is dependent on the player's bet size. For instance, if 6,7,8 suited pays a $100 bonus, then the value in percent will be quite different for a player who has a $2 bet and a player who has a $200 bet. The first player would receive a 50:1 payout on his hand, while the second player would receive only an extra half-bet. The best source book for determining the value of weird bonuses is Stanford Wong's *Basic Blackjack*. All serious players should have this book in their libraries as it defines and provides the strategies for many of the most unusual rules you will encounter in games around the world.

Let's walk through an estimation of our "off the top" expectation in a typical blackjack game. Consider the standard Atlantic City 8-deck game, which allows double after splits, but no resplits. Our basic strategy expectation is derived by adding together the effects of the number of decks in play, and the rule effects (from the multi-deck column). We get:

8 Decks:	-0.57
Double After Splits:	+0.14
No Resplits:	<u>-0.04</u>
House Advantage:	**-0.47**%

3. THE NUMBER OF PLAYERS AT THE TABLE

The third condition you must consider in evaluating the profit potential of a game is the number of players at the table. The more hands you play per hour, assuming you have an advantage, the faster your win rate. If crowded tables keep you from seeing and counting all the cards played, which is a common problem in face-down hand-held games, the effect of this is the same as the effect of an inadequate depth of deal (which is the next table condition we will look at).

Consider, for instance, a single-deck game where there are seven players at the table. Two rounds will consume about 83 percent of the cards, which makes this game appear attractive. Who can complain about 83 percent penetration? Isn't that as good as it gets? But remember that your second (and last) bet before the shuffle will be made after having seen only about 42 percent of the cards, assuming you are able to see and count all cards from the first round. If you are at a table where players are hiding their hands, this cuts further into the amount of usable information you are actually getting on this game.

Let's also consider the effect the number of players at the table has on the speed of the game.

# Players	Hands/Hour
1	200
2	160
3	140
4	120
5	100
6	80
7	65

So, assuming all other factors are equal, including the advantage you are gaining over the house from card counting, and the average amount you are betting per hand, you may expect to win three times as much money per hour if you are going head-to-head with the dealer than if you are playing at a full table.

I do not want to give the impression that I am encouraging you to always play head-to-head. There are many other factors which must enter into this decision. Some team strategies only work well in crowded casinos, and most big money counters find it beneficial to play with other players around, as blending into a crowd is always good camouflage. There is also the simple fact that it is often impossible to find heads-up games in most casinos, as casinos tend to open new tables on an as-needed basis. In analyzing your expected hourly return, however, you must take into account the amount of action you are putting on the tables. This is always strongly affected by the crowd conditions.

4. THE DEPTH OF THE DEAL (PENETRATION)

The final table condition you must consider is the depth of the deal prior to reshuffling. This factor makes no difference whatsoever to basic strategy players. For card counters, penetration is of prime importance. It is usually the major factor in determining whether a game is beatable via card counting or a waste of time. Needless to say, the deeper the penetration, the more profit potential for the counter.

When I published my first book, *The Blackjack Formula,* in 1980, many players were skeptical of the weight I gave to the effect of deck penetration on a card counter's profit potential. I received numerous letters from players who simply could not believe that there could be any great difference in profitability between a single-deck Reno game with 55 percent penetration and one with 65 percent penetration. "Ten percent is only five cards!" one player wrote to me. "Yet your formula shows the advantage almost doubling with the same 1-to-4 spread. That's impossible!" Other card counters, who were playing 4-deck downtown Vegas games with 70 percent penetration and 1-to-4 spreads, were incredulous of my claim that such a small spread, with such poor penetration left them with barely a tenth of a percent advantage over the house.

These days, any decent book on card counting will tell you that penetration is the name of the game. As recently as 1980, no one knew! None of the books on card counting had ever mentioned the importance of deck penetration before.

The general rule is this: The shallower the penetration, the larger the betting spread you must use to beat the game. With a bad set of rules and poor penetration, you may not be able to beat the game with any spread.

In most single-deck games, you cannot win significantly unless more than 50 percent of the cards are dealt out between shuffles. With Reno rules, make that 65 percent. There are two main reasons for this. One, most single-deck games have poor rule sets. Two, you generally cannot get away with a very big spread in single-deck games. With 2-deck games, you'll want better than 60 percent dealt out. But don't even bother with a 2-decker with Reno rules. With 4 or more decks, at least two-thirds (67 percent) of the cards should be dealt out, and this is a bare minimum standard. Most shoe games, in fact, are best attacked by tablehopping, i.e., leaving the game entirely on negative counts. These types of betting strategies are explained in Chapter Ten. Regardless of the number of decks in play, a 10 percent difference in penetration will make a huge difference to your profit potential. A 6-deck game with 85 percent penetration (about 5 decks dealt) is vastly superior to a 6-deck game with only 75 percent penetration (about 4½ decks dealt).

As a basic guideline, *Blackjack Forum* magazine rates penetration as being either good (g), bad (b), or unexceptional (u). Regardless of the number of decks in play, this is what each of the ratings mean:

Bad:	less than 67%
Unexceptional:	67-75%
Good:	76+%

This may be overly simplistic, but if it's all you know, it's a lot more than many who consider themselves smart players. The ability to choose a good game, based on profit potential, is the most powerful weapon of the professional card counter.

♠ ♣ ♥ ♦

7

THE HI-LO LITE

This is an advanced card counting strategy for blackjack players who are willing and able to devote the time and effort necessary to mastering it. It is simpler to learn and play than other true count strategies because the strategy indices have been streamlined for maximum efficiency with minimum effort. Also, the true edge method has been incorporated into both the betting and playing strategies, so that one simple adjustment can be used for all decisions. The recommended exercises for learning how to count cards are the same for the Hi-Lo Lite as for the Red Seven Count, so these exercises will not be repeated here.

I sincerely believe that most players should stick with the Red Seven Count. The Hi-Lo Lite is the counting system I most strongly recommend for dedicated single-deck players, or for shoe players who use shuffle-tracking methods (see Chapter 14). Balanced counting systems can extract significantly more profits from these types of games.

If you are serious enough about blackjack to consider forming or joining a team, then you should know that as counting systems go, the Hi-Lo Count is the *industry standard.* More professionals use the Hi-Lo Count than any other system. Many blackjack teams require that team players use the Hi-Lo Count.

The Hi-Lo Lite is a variation of the standard Hi-Lo Count that uses the same Hi-Lo point values for the cards. I believe the Hi-Lo Lite is a more practical version of the traditional Hi-Lo, easier to learn, easier to play, yet just as strong. Those players who already know the traditional Hi-Lo, and who feel that they can play it easily and without errors, should probably stick with it. But if you are training new players for a team, you may prefer to train these players with the Hi-Lo Lite method. Your team players will train faster, and play with fewer errors. You should also note that the lite indices could easily be converted to traditional count-per-deck indices (just multiply by 2). If you prefer the traditional true count method, due to familiarity, though you would prefer to take advantage of the lite approach to index rounding, then simply adjust the indices for your purposes. You may do this for the purpose of easily learning dozens more indices, either for single-deck opportunities or camouflage plays. If you use shuffle-tracking strategies, there are other advantages to the lite method, which will be discussed in Chapter 14.

THE HI-LO LITE POINT VALUES

The point values of the Hi-Lo Lite Count are:

A:	-1
X:	-1
9:	0
8:	0
7:	0
6:	+1
5:	+1
4:	+1
3:	+1
2:	+1

As the cards are played, the player keeps a running count of all cards seen. After a shuffle, the count always starts at 0. This is a balanced counting system, so if you count down a deck, starting at 0, your final count will return to 0. Because the point values are balanced, it is necessary to adjust your running count to the *true edge.* All Hi-Lo Lite betting and strategy decisions must be made according to the true edge, not the running count.

Important note: If you have not read Chapter Four on the Red Seven Count, then go back *now* and read that chapter, *especially pages 50-54,* which describe the true edge method of running count conversion. *This material is important for Hi-Lo Lite players.* The Hi-Lo Lite uses the same true edge methodology, which differs from the traditional true-count-per-deck method. The true edge method is simply a different method of true count conversion, which I believe to be quicker and easier, *with no loss of accuracy.* In this chapter, I will briefly describe the minor differences between using the true edge method with the Hi-Lo Lite and the Red Seven, but you must read the material in Chapter Four to fully understand the concept.

As with the Advanced Red Seven Count, we estimate our true edge with the Hi-Lo Lite by dividing the running count by twice the number of remaining decks. Example: you are in a 6-deck game and one deck has been played. Your running count is +15. Your true edge is:

$$\frac{15}{5 \ (remaining \ decks) \times 2} = \frac{15}{10} = 1\frac{1}{2}\%$$

This means that the +15 running count at this point in the shoe indicates that your edge has risen about 1½ percent above your (dis)advantage off the top of the shoe.

Note that with the Hi-Lo Lite, both our starting count and our pivot = 0, so our pivot advantage is always the same as our advantage off the top. When we used the true edge method with the Red Seven Count, our pivot advantage was always positive, and about 1 percent higher than our starting advantage. So, the difference between using the true edge method with the Hi-Lo Lite and the Red Seven is that with the Red Seven we are usually adding the true edge to a *positive pivot advantage,* usually around ½ percent, and with the Hi-Lo Lite, we add our true edge to the starting advantage off the top, which is usually about -½ percent.

In the example above, if this were a 6-deck Atlantic City game, which is -½ percent off the top, then the 1½ percent gain would indicate a total advantage of about an even 1 percent.

Another example: same game, a few minutes later, 2 decks have been played and your running count is -4. Your true edge is:

$$\frac{-4}{4 \ (remaining \ decks) \times 2} = \frac{-4}{8} = -\frac{1}{2}\%$$

The true edge method differs from the more common true count methodology used for most balanced counting systems, as we are directly figuring out the approximate gain or loss in our advantage as we make the true edge conversion. I have decided to use this methodology for the Hi-Lo Lite for a number of reasons. As explained in Chapter Four, I think it is simpler and more convenient to estimate the raise in your edge directly. Since the true edge method works so easily with the Advanced Red Seven, it will also make it easier for Red Seven players to switch over to the Hi-Lo Lite when they are ready.

With the Hi-Lo Lite, we will also use the true edge method for making our playing strategy decisions. The traditional true count methodology is to divide your running count by the number of decks remaining. This may sound easy, but when your running count is +11, and 2½ decks remain, what's your true count? Many players are stumped when they try to divide by half decks, especially with odd-numbered running counts. When you're trying to make a decision quickly, you don't need this aggravation. With the above example and the true edge method, in an instant you come up with the fraction 11/5, and you know your edge has risen slightly more than 2 percent.

The Hi-Lo Lite Playing Strategy

As you will note from the Hi-Lo Lite strategy charts, all of the index numbers are in even numbered percentages, making precision play easier than ever. The Hi-Lo Lite allows you to play your cards, varying from basic strategy, with a high degree of accuracy. The strategy changes presented here provide most of the gains available from the Hi-Lo Lite system. You may use these indices for any number of decks, and any set of rules. In shoe games, you only need the **bold** "Sweet 16" and "Fab 4" surrender indices (as per Don Schlesinger's *Blackjack Attack).* If you play in games where the dealer hits soft 17, you will find these indices, along with many other less important indices, in the Appendix. *Use basic strategy for all decisions for which no index number is provided.*

To use the chart on page 76:

Stand only when your true edge is equal to or greater than the number in the table.

Double down only when your true edge is equal to or greater than the number in the table. Note that no soft doubling indices are provided here. There is very little value to varying from basic strategy on soft doubling decisions. If you want to use these indices, you will find them in the Appendix.

Split all pairs according to *basic strategy.* A few of the ten splits have some dollar value, but these are not advisable for card counters. (See Chapter 12 on camouflage.) There is very little dollar value to varying from basic strategy on other pair split de-

THE HI-LO LITE
USE FOR ANY NUMBER OF DECKS
ASSUMES STAND ON SOFT 17

	2	3	4	5	6	7	8	9	X	A
STAND										
16						4	4	**2**	**0**	4
15	-2							4	**2**	
14	-2	-2	-2							
13	**0**	**0**	-2	-2	-2					
12	**2**	**0**	**0**	**0**	**0**					
DOUBLE DOWN										
11							-2	-2	-2	**0**
10						-2	-2	0	**2**	**2**
9	**0**	0	0	-2	-2	**2**	4			
8		4	2	2	0					
SURRENDER										
16							2	0	0	0
8-8								4	0	
15							4	**2**	**0**	**0**
14								4	**2**	4
7-7								2	2	2
13									4	

INSURANCE: **2**

BOLD = Sweet 16 + Fab 4

cisions. You will find extensive pair split indices, which may have some camouflage value, in the Appendix. Learn these if you want, but they are worth very little in dollars and cents.

Surrender only when your true edge is equal to or greater than the number in the table. Note that these are the late surrender indices. Should you discover an early surrender game (rare), you will find the proper indices in the Appendix.

Take *insurance* only when your true edge is equal to or greater than the number in the table.

The easiest way to learn the Hi-Lo Lite strategy indices is to start with the bold "Sweet 16" and learn these indices in blocks.

Unless you play in games with surrender, you may ignore the bold "Fab 4" for surrender.

The 0-Block **16 v. X** **13 v. 2 & 3** **12 v. 3,4,5 & 6** **11 v. A** **9 v. 2**	**The +2-Block** **16 v. 9** **15 v. X** **12 v. 2** **10 v. X & A** **9 v. 7** **Insurance**

The 0-Block is most important. After you learn these, learn the +2-Block. *Shoe game players need never learn any indices other than these.* If you play in hand-held games, these 16 indices, which Don Schlesinger calls the "Sweet Sixteen," are still the most important. Learn the others in blocks, if you want to add an extra few tenths of a percent to your advantage, starting with the positive indices. The negative indices are least important.

Players who are familiar with traditional Hi-Lo strategy tables, or for that matter, with true count strategy tables for any balanced card counting system, will be shocked by the simplicity of the Hi-Lo Lite. Many experts will doubt its strength and playing accuracy. Allow me to describe the history of its development.

Early in 1991, I attempted to answer via high-speed computer simulation whether Stanford Wong's or Julian Braun's version of the Hi-Lo Count was more accurate. Both were respected programmers and blackjack authorities who had devised indices for the Hi-Lo Count which differed on dozens of decisions. Using John Imming's *Universal Blackjack Engine* software, I ran off 500 million hands of each strategy with a flat bet in single-deck games with Vegas Strip rules, using all indices between -15 and +15. At the end of the test, Wong's indices bettered Braun's result by .009 percent (less than one-hundredth of one percent), but this was within 2 standard errors, not a statistically significant result.

My simulation results led me to theorize that strategy index numbers may not be such precise indicators of when to alter basic strategy, or at least, that the borderline for the coin-toss decisions may be a fairly wide line. I set up another test to see just how wide that borderline might be. I simulated a 6-deck Atlantic City game and ran off 200 million hands using Wong's *Professional Blackjack* indices (Illustrious 18 only). For the second simulation, I converted each of Wong's indices to -1, +1 or +4. I did this systematically; if Wong's index was -1 or -2, I made it -1. If he had an index of 0, +1 or +2, I made it +1. His +3, +4, and +5 indices all became +4. I then ran off another 200 million hands testing this simplified version of Wong's strategy. In both simulations, I used a 1-to-8 spread, and I also tested the effect of not betting on negative counts.

These were the results:

Strategy	**Play All**	**No Neg.**
Wong	+0.50%	+0.98%
Simplified	+0.51%	+0.99%

In a test of 200 million hands, the fact that the simplified version of the Hi-Lo outperformed the exact version by .01 percent is not mathematically significant. What is significant is that such an approximate version of the Hi-Lo strategy performs with *equal power* to the precise version.

I wondered how well this approach would work in single-deck games where playing strategy is so much more important? So, I set up a Reno one-deck simulation, and used 60 indices from Wong's *Professional Blackjack*. I ran 100 million hands, and tallied the results with both a flat bet and a 1-to-4 spread at 75% penetration. This time, in the "lite" version of the Hi-Lo, I widened the border again, converting all of Wong's indices to plus or minus 1, 5, or 10. The results:

Strategy	**Flat Bet**	**1-to-4**
Wong	-0.06%	+1.32%
Hi-Lo Lite	-0.05%	+1.33%

The fact that the Lite system outperformed Wong's by one-hundredth of one percent again is not significant in a test of 100 million hands. What is important is that from the practical, dollars and cents, perspective, it doesn't matter which of these systems you use. The simulation results indicate that you may use a vastly simplified Hi-Lo strategy, and maintain full power, even in a one-deck game.

So, in 1991, I published a series of three articles in *Casino Player* magazine about this astonishing discovery. I developed the Hi-Lo Lite counting system to be a feature of the revised *Blackbelt in Blackjack,* which I intended to publish in 1992 (six years ago!). Then, in October of 1991, the Oakland Firestorm destroyed the manuscript, so I published the Hi-Lo Lite without much fanfare in the December 1991 issue of *Blackjack Forum.* Since that time, I have been personally advising players to simplify their strategy charts with this lite approach.

John Imming later discovered the reason why the lite approach to indices works so well. In attempting to determine why his *Universal Blackjack Engine* software sometimes devised different indices for the same counting system via simulations of hundreds of millions of hands, Imming discovered that the actual indices were not precise, but constantly wavered according to the level of penetration and other factors. Some indices went up and down by a few numbers until finally settling.

Last year, Ken Fuchs, co-author of *Knock-Out Blackjack,* presented a paper at the 10th International Gambling Conference in which his simulation results of a slightly different lite counting system supported my findings. Then, George C. privately devised a lite version of the Zen Count, which John Auston tested against the regular Zen indices using the *Statistical Blackjack Analyzer* software. It took Auston *a billion hands* of each system to determine that the lite indices underperformed the regular indices by about two-hundredths of one percent.

It was George C., incidentally, who discovered that all of the +1 and -1 lite indices could be adjusted to 0, with no notable loss of power. So, the version of the Hi-Lo Lite published here has been further simplified in this regard. If you want to test the Hi-Lo Lite via computer simulations of your own, note that the *true edge* methodology is *not* the same as *true-count-per-deck.* If your blackjack simulation program does not allow you to enter indices as *true-count-per-half-deck,* then you must double the Hi-Lo Lite indices. For the Sweet 16, all indices are either 0 or +4. I.e., to fully adjust the complete chart, make all +2s into +4s, -4s into -8s, etc., in order to test the system with a count-per-deck simulator.

♠ ♣ ♥ ♦

8

THE ZEN COUNT

This is a level-two, balanced card counting strategy for blackjack players who are above average in counting talent. If you can use the Zen Count accurately, it will add about 0.1 percent to your advantage in shoe games, and in single-deck games, about 0.2 percent to what you would expect with the Hi-Lo Lite. The recommended drills for learning how to count cards are the same for the Zen Count as for the Red Seven Count or the Hi-Lo Lite, so these exercises will not be repeated here.

THE ZEN COUNT POINT VALUES

The point values of the Zen Count are:

A:	-1
X:	-2
9:	0
8:	0
7:	+1
6:	+2
5:	+2
4:	+2
3:	+1
2:	+1

As the cards are played, the player keeps a running count of all cards seen. After a shuffle, the count starts again at 0. Like the Hi-Lo Lite, this is a balanced counting system, so if you count down a complete deck, starting at 0, your final count will return to 0. Because the point values are balanced, it is necessary to adjust your running count to the true edge. All Zen Count betting and playing strategy decisions must be made according to the true edge, not the running count.

Because the Zen Count is a level-two counting system, with more complex point values than the Red Seven or Hi-Lo Lite, we must estimate our true edge by dividing our running count by the number of remaining decks times 4 (instead of times 2). Otherwise, we use the same make-a-fraction method, in which our running count is the numerator, and the denominator is 4 x the number of remaining decks. In order to do this quickly at the tables, you must memorize the following chart:

Decks Remaining	Denominator
8	32
7	28
6	24
5	20
4	16
3	12
2	8
1	4
½	2

I think most players who remember their 4 times tables from third grade could reproduce this chart with no memory work whatsoever. It is important that you are able to *immediately* insert this denominator into your fraction so that your true edge does not require you to be making calculations at the table. If your running count is +7 with 3 decks remaining to be dealt, you should immediately know that your true edge has risen by 7/12, or slightly more than ½ percent.

With a running count of +19, and 2 decks remaining, the true edge is 19/8, or almost a 2½ percent raise from the starting advantage. If you have any trouble with fractions like these, for instance, if you do not know fairly quickly that 19/8 is about 2½, then you should *not* be using the Zen Count. I would suggest that you stick with the simple Red Seven, and play according to running count. In my opinion, the true edge method is the easiest method of adjusting a running count to estimate your advantage with precision, but not all players are comfortable with this math.

In the first half of the shoe, you will not lose any accuracy if you estimate the remaining decks to the nearest whole deck by always rounding *up*. For example, if my running count is +10, and 5½ decks remain to be dealt, if I round up to 6 decks, then make the fraction 11/24, this is easy and accurate enough for bet sizing purposes. It is clear that my advantage has risen slightly less than ½ percent. Technically, with 5½ decks remaining, it would be more accurate to use the denominator 22, halfway between 5 and 6 decks remaining. My true edge is more precisely 11/22, or exactly a ½ percent raise. The real difference between 11/24 and 11/22, however, is so small that it is unlikely to have any affect on my bet size.

Deeper in the shoe, however, as the denominators get smaller, the effect of rounding the remaining decks up to the nearest full deck will have more of an effect. For instance in the example on the previous page, with a running count of +19 and 2 decks remaining, we came up with the fraction 19/8, or just under 2½. If the actual decks remaining were only 1½ (which we rounded up to 2), our actual fraction would more accurately have been 19/6, which is slightly better than 3 percent.

Again, this is more important when there are fewer than 4 decks remaining. You will note from the above example that by rounding up from 1½ to 2 decks, we would tend to bet *more conservatively,* which is better than rounding down, and overbetting. Some players may want to make a chart of denominators in half-deck increments, but I doubt this is necessary. If you know that your 4-deck denominator is 16, and your 3-deck denominator is 12, it would probably not take more than an instant for you to come up with a denominator of 14 if you estimated that 3½ decks remained to be dealt.

In single-deck games (or in any mutiple-deck game which is played down into the last deck), the most accurate method of true edge adjustment is to consider the deck as four distinct quarters. In the first quarter, your true edge is your running count divided by 4. In the second quarter, your true edge is your running count divided by 3. In the third quarter, your true edge is your running count divided by 2. And in the bottom quarter, your true edge *is your running count* (i.e., a running count of +6 with a quarter deck or less remaining to be dealt would indicate a 6 percent raise in your advantage).

Incidentally, Zen Count players who are already familiar with the count-per-deck method presented in the first edition of this book may choose to continue with that method. The true edge method is simply a *count-per-quarter-deck* adjustment,

THE ZEN STRATEGY
USE FOR ANY NUMBER OF DECKS
ASSUMES STAND ON SOFT 17

	2	3	4	5	6	7	8	9	X	A
				STAND						
16							4	**2**	**0**	3
15	-2							4	**1**	4
14	-1	-2	-2						3	
13	**0**	**-1**	-1	-2	-2					
12	**1**	**1**	**0**	**-1**	**0**					
				DOUBLE DOWN						
11								-2	-2	**0**
10							-2	-1	**1**	**1**
9	**0**	0	-1	-2		**2**	4			
8		4	3	2	1					
				SURRENDER						
16							2	0	-2	-1
8-8								4	0	
15							3	**1**	**0**	**1**
14							4	2	**1**	2
7-7									1	
13									3	

INSURANCE: **1**

BOLD = Sweet 16 + Fab 4

which will always provide you with your true edge when you use the make-a-fraction technique. I think it is very practical to always know your advantage quickly while you play. You might also note that the Zen true edge playing strategy chart is much simpler than the old count-per-deck chart. In fact, it is very similar to the Hi-Lo Lite chart.

THE ZEN COUNT PLAYING STRATEGY

The strategy changes presented here provide most of the gains available from the Zen Count system. You may use these indices for any number of decks, and any set of rules. In shoe games, you only need the **bold** "Sweet 16" and "Fab 4" surrenders (as per Don Schlesinger's *Blackjack Attack)*. If you play in games where the dealer hits soft 17, you will find these indices, along with many other less important indices, in the Appendix. *Use basic strategy for all decisions for which no index number is provided.*

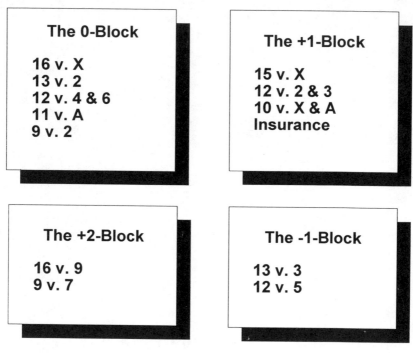

The 0-Block

16 v. X
13 v. 2
12 v. 4 & 6
11 v. A
9 v. 2

The +1-Block

15 v. X
12 v. 2 & 3
10 v. X & A
Insurance

The +2-Block

16 v. 9
9 v. 7

The -1-Block

13 v. 3
12 v. 5

To use the chart on page 83:

Stand only when your true edge is equal to or greater than the number in the table.

Double down only when your true edge is equal to or greater than the number in the table. Note that no soft doubling indices are provided here. There is very little value to varying from basic strategy on soft doubling decisions. If you want to use these indices, you will find them in the Appendix.

Split all pairs according to *basic strategy*. A few of the ten splits have some dollar value, but these are not advisable for card counters. (See Chapter 12 on camouflage.) There is very little dollar value to varying from basic strategy on other pair split decisions. You will find extensive pair split indices, which may have some camouflage value, in the Appendix. Learn these if you want, but they are worth very little in dollars and cents.

Surrender only when your true edge is equal to or greater than the number in the table. Note that these are the late surrender indices. Should you discover an early surrender game (rare), you will find the proper indices in the Appendix.

Take *insurance* only when your true edge is equal to or greater than the number in the table.

The easiest way to learn the Zen strategy indices is to start with the bold "Sweet 16" and learn these indices in blocks. Unless you play in games with surrender, you may also ignore the bold "Fab 4" for surrender.

The 0-Block is most important. After you learn these, learn the +1-Block, then the +2-Block, and finally, the -1-Block. *Shoe game players need never learn any indices other than these.* If you play in hand-held games, these 16 indices, which Don Schlesinger calls the "Sweet Sixteen," are still the most important. Learn the others in blocks, if you want to add an extra few tenths of a percent to your advantage, starting with the positive indices. The negative indices are least important.

If you want to test the Zen Count system as presented here via computer simulations, and your blackjack simulation program does not allow you to enter indices as *true-count-per-quarter-deck,* then you must multiply all of the Zen indices by 4, in order to use a traditional count per deck adjustment. For the Sweet 16, the -1, +1, and +2 indices become -4, +4, and +8, respectively.

9

TRUE COUNT

WHAT IS TRUE COUNT?

Definition: True count is an adjusted running count which indicates the balance of high cards to low cards. True count is, in fact, not "true" as a precise indicator of your advantage. But it does reflect the balance of the cards so that you may approximate both your advantage and your playing strategy.

Most level-one systems, like the Hi-Lo, recommend that true count be estimated as count per deck. The true edge with the Hi-Lo Lite is simply the count per half-deck. Some authors who have developed higher level counting systems, most notably Ken Uston and Lawrence Revere, have advised count-per-half-deck adjustments. With the Zen Count, the true edge method is actually a count per quarter-deck.

Take a full 52-card deck. Count the point value of all the tens and aces using the Zen Count. With 16 tens and 4 aces, the points add up to -36. If you now count all of the points of the low cards, 2's, 3's, 4's, 5's, 6's and 7's, you'll find that these add up to +36. The deck is perfectly balanced:

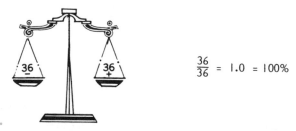

$$\frac{36}{36} = 1.0 = 100\%$$

Now, let's remove 8 tens and 2 aces from the deck. Adding up the point values of the high cards remaining in the deck, we now get -18. Our balance looks like this:

$$\frac{18}{36} = .50 = 50\%$$

The deck is heavy in low cards and light in high cards.

There are, in fact, exactly one half (or 50%) as many high card points as low card points in the remaining deck.

If this situation occurred at a blackjack table, i.e., if 8 tens and 2 aces had been played in the first round of hands, and no low cards came out of the deck, the running count would be -18

But consider what the balance would look like if this situation occurred while playing a 6-deck shoe game. To start with, six full decks contain 96 tens and 24 aces. The high card points balanced against the low card points look like this:

Now, if we remove 8 tens and 2 aces, our balance looks like this:

$$\frac{198}{216} = .92 = 92\%$$

The balance is only slightly tipped because there were so many more points to start with. Although the same cards have been removed as in our single-deck example, we still have 92% as many high card points as low card points in the shoe. What this means to the card counter is that although his running count may be -18 in both situations, his advantage, and his playing strategy, would differ. The running count must be adjusted to reflect the true balance of high cards to low cards.

TRUE COUNT BY DIVISION

The most common method of determining true count is to divide the running count by the number of remaining decks (or half-decks). The chief difficulty of this method is that it often involves dividing by fractions. The true edge methods I propose solve this problem. Other methods may be used.

THE "TRUE INDEX" METHOD

For strategy variations, instead of adjusting your running count, you may find it easier to adjust your index number to the *true index* at which you would alter your basic strategy. This method works well for players who are not comfortable working with fractions.

With the Hi-Lo Lite you simply multiply the index number of the decision in question by the number of remaining half-decks, then compare this number to the running count. For instance, let's say you are trying to decide whether or not to take insurance in a 6-deck game with a running count of +9. Four decks have been played, so 2 remain. Since your Hi-Lo insurance index number is +2, you compute your true index by multiplying +2 x 4 (remaining half-decks) = +8. And you would take insurance here because your running count of +9 is higher than the true index.

With the Zen Count, you would multiply your index by the number of quarter-decks remaining. Your insurance index is +1 with Zen, so +1 x 8 quarter-decks = +8, and again a +9 running count would indicate an insurance bet.

This method may be used for all strategy decisions. To do it quickly, you must *instantly* know the number of half-decks (or quarter-decks) remaining. With the Zen Count, it would be wise to learn the number of quarter decks in half-deck increments, so that when you have a situation with 2½ decks remaining, you know that you must multiply your index number by 10 to get the true index. For some players, this would be very easy, and would require no memory work.

THE "TRUE SHOE" METHOD

To use this method of true count adjustment, you simply divide your running count (which is always a whole number) by the index number of the decision you are considering (also always a whole number), and the answer is the number of half-decks (or quarter decks with Zen) *or fewer* which must be remaining for you to make the play. For example, your Hi-Lo running count is +10 and you want to know whether you should stand on your hard total of 12 vs. a dealer 2. Your standing index number for this decision is +2. Simply divide the running count +10 by 2 = 5, and if 5 half-decks (2½ decks) or *fewer* remain, you would stand. In order to justify this strategy deviation, with this running count, your *true shoe* size must be 2½ decks or fewer. Otherwise, follow basic strategy and hit.

The easiest way to use the true shoe method, with any counting system, would be to first convert all strategy indices to count per deck. This way your running count divided by your index always results in the true number of decks remaining, instead of half or quarter-decks, where the decision changes.

Note: If your running count is negative and your index number is positive, or vice versa, don't bother to make any true count adjustment using any method. Follow basic strategy.

ESTIMATING THE REMAINING DECKS

One art you will have to perfect, regardless of your method of true count adjustment, is estimating the number of remaining decks. You cannot do this without practice.

Buy yourself a few dozen decks of standard playing cards. Use casino-quality cards, preferably used (good quality) cards obtained from a casino, so that the thickness of the decks is the same as you will encounter in casino play. Many casinos sell their used decks in their gift shops. Make up stacks of cards containing 8 decks, 7½ decks, 7, 6½, 5½, 5, 4½, 4, 3½, 3, 2½, 2, 1½, 1 and ½. (You will need to purchase 62 decks of cards to make up all of these stacks. Believe me, pros do it.) Familiarize yourself with exactly what each sized stack looks like.

In a casinos, you won't be looking at such exactly sized stacks of discards very often, but your eyes will estimate to the nearest sized stack with which you have familiarized yourself so that you may make your adjustments effortlessly.

Never waste a moment in this estimation process. If it appears 2¼ decks are remaining, call it 2½. Always round *up*. This way you'll play more conservatively. Call it 2 only when it's definitely below 2¼.

Also, when you eyeball one of your practice stacks, remember that you are looking at the *discards*. Therefore, if you are assuming you are in a 6-deck game, and you look at a stack of 4 decks, you will be making your true count adjustment based on 2 decks — *the remaining decks.* Be sure you practice this way.

True count adjustment is one of the most difficult aspects of card counting to master. Most counters are ill-trained in this area and should stick with the running count systems.

If you ever try to join a professional blackjack team, don't be surprised if you are tested rigorously on true count adjustments. The team captain will likely show you various-sized stacks of discards and give you hypothetical strategy decisions. He will expect you to respond with the proper plays immediately, based on your system. After each response, you'll have to explain in detail the methodology you followed in making your decision.

I'm always surprised by the sloppy, slow, and ill-trained players who believe they would be winning fortunes if they just had the big bankroll behind them. They often complain about cheating dealers, poor conditions, negative fluctuations, etc. But they are using systems beyond their abilities, and can't make accurate decisions to save their lives. These players, and the majority of card counters fall into this group, are the meat and potatoes of the casino industry.

♠ ♣ ♥ ♦

10

BETTING STRATEGIES

There is one concept behind all betting strategies for card counters: bet more when you have the edge, and less (or nothing) when the house has the edge.

A number of factors complicate this dictum. First, you must know how much more to bet when you have the edge. Second, you must raise your bet so that you do not attract attention to yourself. Third, your bankroll must be sufficient to withstand the fluctuations.

Serious players, who intend to devote any substantial amount of time or money to the pursuit of blackjack profits, must go beyond the scope of this book for a more comprehensive education in the mathematics of risk. At the very least, you should study Don Schlesinger's *Blackjack Attack,* which covers this topic more thoroughly than any other source.

Most card counters, who are playing primarily for the sport of it, should find the information provided herein adequate. My approach is conservative, as I feel this is wiser for casual players. Players who use the simple Red Seven, or for that matter any unbalanced card counting system which does not include a true edge adjustment, must bet more conservatively than players who are using an accurate method of estimating their advantage as they play.

SINGLE-DECK BETTING STRATEGIES

In single-deck games, your high bet with the simple Red Seven should be your total bankroll divided by 100. Given a $2,000 bankroll, your high bet should be $20. This assumes that you are using the simplified betting chart on page 46, with a 1-to-8 spread. In actual play, you may find it impractical or impossible to spread 1-to-8 with a $20 maximum bet. I don't think most casinos would accept the $2.50 minimum bet. If you can find a table that has a $3.00 minimum, you could spread $3-to-20, which is almost 1-to-7. But in many casinos, you'll be stuck with a 1-to-4 spread, or $5-to-20. In this case, note that you do not want to place your maximum $20 bet until your count justifies the 8-unit bet according to the page 45 betting chart. Otherwise, you will be placing far too many $20 bets when you do not have a sufficient advantage to justify them.

You must constantly reassess the size of your bankroll as you play, and alter the size of your bets accordingly. This need not be a difficult accounting procedure. You know the size of your bankroll prior to beginning play. Now keep track of how much money you pull out of your pocket as you play.

Always buy chips in small amounts. If you're playing with nickels ($5 chips), don't buy in for more than $100. If you're playing with quarters ($25 chips), you need not buy in for more than $500. If you need more chips, you can always pull more money out of your pocket. Pit bosses are sometimes wary of players who buy in for large amounts, then start betting small. Casino floormen like to see players digging into their pockets for more money since this indicates the player has been losing. By keeping track of how much money you pull from your pocket, you'll always know your bankroll position. The difference is right in front of your eyes. When there is a significant change in your bankroll, divide by 100 to redetermine the size of your high bet. Most of the time, you will approximate this bet size. For instance, with a $3,150 bankroll, your optimal high bet would be:

$$\$3,150 \,/\, 100 = \$31.50$$

Your high bet would be $30. Remember that you will experience wild swings of positive and negative fluctuations. On occasion, you may have to reassess your bankroll after only 10 minutes of play. If you fail to reassess your bankroll often enough, it could be devastating to you in a few hours. You must cut back when you lose, and you must do it quickly. Try to reassess after winning or losing ten high bets. With a high bet of $25, you should stop and reassess after winning or losing about $250. Again, if you keep track of how much cash you've pulled out of your pocket, this is automatic.

The betting spread you need to beat a game depends on the rules of that game and what percentage of the cards you are able to see and count. One of the best guides for choosing a single-deck game was produced by Brother William. He noted that many casinos instructed their dealers to deal a specified number of rounds between shuffles, based on the number of players at the table. In order to get a one percent advantage over the house, using the simple Red Seven, based on the number of rounds between shuffles and the number of players at the table, these are the required betting spreads:

Rounds	Number of Players						
	1	2	3	4	5	6	7
One	-	-	-	-	-	-	-
	-	-	-	-	-	-	-
Two	-	-	-	-	-	1-8	1-6
	-	-	-	-	*1-8*	*1-5*	*1-4*
Three	-	-	1-6	1-4			
	-	-	*1-4*	*1-3*			
Four	-	1-8	1-4				
	-	*1-6*	*1-3*				
Five	1-8	1-4					
	1-6	*1-3*					
Six	1-5						
	1-4						
Seven	1-4						
	1-3						
Eight	1-3						
	1-2						

In each row, the top spread is for Reno rules, where dealers hit soft 17, and you may double down on 10 and 11 only. The spreads below, *in italics,* are for downtown Vegas rules, where the dealers hit soft 17, but you may double on any two cards.

Assuming there are only two players at the table, and you are playing vs. Reno rules, if the dealer is dealing only four rounds between shuffles, then you will need a 1-8 spread in order to get a one percent advantage. Note that if there were three players at the table, and four rounds, you could get this 1 percent advantage with only a 1-4 spread.

Red Seven players should use this chart as a guide to choosing single-deck games. If you cannot get a 1 percent advantage because the dealer is dealing too few rounds, don't play. Find a better game. Note that the five-player game is extremely poor. With Reno rules, you cannot beat it (unless you spread bigger than 1-to-8!). Five players with two rounds is very poor, and no dealer will attempt to deal a third round with five players at the table. The best games are three rounds to four players, or four rounds to three players.

Advanced Red Seven players, who are using the extra indices provided for single-deck games, as well as Hi-Lo Lite and Zen players, will find many more single-deck games of value, and with smaller spreads. As a general guide, if you are using the sweet sixteen indices, assume that you could beat either the Reno or downtown Vegas game spreading one unit less than in the page 93 chart. If you are using the full set of indices provided for the Hi-Lo Lite or Zen Count, you may spread two units less than the spreads recommended in the chart. Strategy plays have great value in single-deck games.

If you use the Red Seven Count, you raise your bet from the minimum at the pivot (0). If you use the Hi-Lo Lite or Zen Count, raise your bet when the edge has turned to your favor by at least ½ percent (see Chapters Seven and Eight). Unless you're a good actor, you should stick with the lowest recommended betting spreads in single-deck games. A wider spread will increase your win rate, but it will also increase your chance of being identified as a card counter.

Players who make bets above $50 might be wise to avoid single-deck games altogether, or at least until you have a better feel for casino play, and getting away with card counting. At low stakes (all bets below $50), many casinos ignore spreads of 1-to-4 or even 1-to-8, but don't take unnecessary chances. Some casinos will tolerate no counters at all at their tables. If you sense heat, leave and play elsewhere. Return another day, or on another shift.

If your total bankroll is under $5,000, you would also be wise to employ "one-deck Wonging," a betting strategy described in Chapter Ten.

Two-Deck Games

Two-deck games are common in Nevada. Calculate your high bet for 2-deck games as your bankroll divided by 120. With Reno rules, play in one-deck games only, which are commonly available. Do not play two-deckers with Reno rules. You can beat these games if there is 75 percent penetration, and you use a 1-8 spread, but much better games are available in Northern Nevada. In Las Vegas, play in 2-deck games only if at least 60 percent of the cards are dealt out between shuffles. You must use at least a 1-to-5 spread to get a 1 percent edge at these games. With more favorable rules, and a deeper shuffle point, you can get a stronger advantage, or use a smaller spread.

These recommendations are based on extensive computer simulations of the simple six-index Red Seven by Brother William, as well as by John Auston for the Hi-Lo, the Red Seven, and the Zen Count, all using the "Illustrious 18" indices.

Four-or-More-Deck Games

For all shoe games, estimate your high best as your bankroll divided by 150. When you are playing vs. four or more decks, frequent tablehopping is generally a good idea. You want to leave the table on negative counts. This technique is often called "Wonging" by card counters, after blackjack pro Stanford Wong, who popularized this playing style. Wonging is simply refusing to play vs. negative situations. When your count indicates that the house has any significant edge, you leave the table to find a better game. On the first couple of rounds after a shuffle, you may tolerate a low negative running count. After the first half-deck or so is in the discard tray, stay only if the count is neutral or plus. If you are in a large casino and there are many open table opportunities, do not play vs. any negative running count.

Your best approach to tablehopping is to keep your eyes open as you walk through the blackjack pits. Look for dealers who are shuffling, finishing a shuffle, or just beginning a new deal (with very few cards in the discard tray). When you spot a crowded table with an open betting spot or two, and the felt gets covered with low (plus) cards, get as accurate a count as you can, and get a bet, or bets, onto any open betting spaces. If you are using the Red Seven Count, you are seeking tables with running counts at, or close to, your pivot. In 6 and 8-deck games, you will rarely hit your pivot in one round of play. But if the count goes beyond the halfway point, either watch the next round, or get a small waiting bet on the table. The Red Seven Count is particularly powerful for this playing style. Its betting efficiency is high, and all of its variations from basic strategy are plus-count variations. If you are using a true edge adjustment, you are seeking tables where your true count indicates that you have the advantage. This will depend on the number of decks, rules, etc.

When tablehopping, you will sometimes walk for long periods without placing a bet. You will sometimes play only one hand before the count goes down again. For this reason, it's best to cover two (or more) betting spots when you find an advantageous betting situation.

Your tablehopping must appear natural or you will be recognized as a card counter. You cannot stand behind a table and count round after round, jumping in only when the count goes up. This is too obvious. You must appear casual. Tablehopping is probably easiest to pull off when you are with a companion of the opposite sex. While searching for good tables, you can act like you're more interested in each other, wandering around like lovers at a carnival.

In Atlantic City, many casinos prohibit tablehopping by disallowing mid-shoe entry. Some casinos may restrict bets to the table minimum of any player who enters a game after the first round from a shuffle. These rules are specifically designed to foil Wonging. In casinos where such rules are enforced, the only way to tablehop is to enter games right after the shuffle, stay if the count goes up, and leave if it goes down, in search of another newly shuffled shoe. No card counting strategy can significantly beat a six- or eight-deck game if less than 65 percent of the cards are dealt out, unless you are allowed to tablehop. Even with tablehopping, less than 65 percent penetration will provide little profit potential for card counters.

When tablehopping, you may either use a betting spread or flat bet. Flat-betting will work only if you wait until you have a decided edge until entering a game. Otherwise, you must spread your bets, at least 1-to-4 units, and often higher. Remember to only raise your bet after a win, by parlaying. If you attempt raising after a loss, you must appear to be chasing your losses, as a compulsive gambler might. To pull this off, you may have to make comments to the dealer or other players about "feeling a winning streak coming up," "ending a losing streak," etc. Many of the most successful card counters are those who can convince the casinos that they are die-hard gamblers. Some of these players use phenomenal betting spreads, sometimes 1-to-40 units and more, by being good actors.

If you use a true edge adjustment, remember when adjusting your running count that this adjustment is based on *unseen cards*. If you enter a 6-deck game in progress after counting only one round, you must keep aware of the fact that you have seen and counted very few cards. There may be half a deck or more already in the discard pile. Do not make your true edge adjustments by estimating that you have seen all the discards.

The rules are very important to card counters in shoe games. Surrender is worth about a quarter of a percent to a counter who is using a large spread. Double after splits is worth just a bit less. With both of these rules on the game, your count strategy will be worth almost half a percent more than without these rules. That is a huge difference.

A card counter recently asked me if he could beat shoe games without tablehopping if he used a 1-12 spread. This may sound like a simple question, but the answer is quite complicated. How many decks? What's the penetration? What are the rules? Let's look at the player advantages (in percent) from John Auston's "World's Greatest Blackjack Simulation" report for the Red Seven Count, using a 1-12 spread in both 6 and 8-deck games, with three different (but common) levels of penetration, and three different rule sets: dealer hits soft 17 (H17); dealer stands on soft 17 (S17); and dealer stands on soft 17 plus late surrender (S17-LS).

	H17	**S17**	**S17-LS**
6 Decks, 67% Penetration	0.39	0.71	0.99
6 Decks, 75% Penetration	0.79	1.16	1.53
6 Decks, 83% Penetration	1.31	1.68	2.07
8 Decks, 69% Penetration	-0.04	0.27	0.50
8 Decks, 75% Penetration	0.18	0.49	0.76
8 Decks, 81% Penetration	0.44	0.77	1.10

So, despite the fact that in all cases the player is using a 1-12 spread in all of these games, with the same counting system, his expectation ranges from -0.04 percent to 2.07 percent! Notice how important all three variables — number of decks, penetration, and rules — are to the expectation. This is why most pros use computer simulation software themselves to test games and betting approaches. If you don't have a computer to run your own simulations, there are now books available (such as Auston's) that contain nothing but hundreds of charts of simulation data, comparing different games with different table conditions. If you intend to put any serious amount of money into this game, you have to invest a bit in your education.

Multi-deck games also restrict profitable playing opportunities for players with limited bankrolls. For example, suppose you find a 6-deck Vegas Strip game with 4 decks dealt (a 67 percent shuffle-point). Note in the chart that with a 1-12 spread, your expectation is 0.71 percent. If you want a full 1 percent advantage in this game, you'll have to spread 1-16. Since the table minimum bet is $2, you must spread your bets from $2 to $32. Since, for 6-deck games, your high bet is optimally your bankroll divided by 150, then in order to make this high bet of $32, you would have to have at least 150 x $32 = $4,800. So, if you don't have $5,000 to play with, you can't beat this game sufficiently because you can't afford a $2 betting unit!

The only way to compensate for this, if you do not have a sufficient bankroll, is to play less frequently under unfavorable circumstances. Tablehop. Tablehop. Tablehop. (Of course, the best solution is to find a better game. Six decks with only four dealt sucks!) The difficulty with tablehopping a game like this is that you may not find enough betting situations to be worth the time spent looking.

PLAYING SIMULTANEOUS HANDS

When you are tablehopping, you will often want to place bets on more than one spot at a time. When the count is relatively neutral, a single bet is all you want on the table, but as your expectation rises, multiple simultaneous hands are often desirable because they will camouflage your spread, and let you get more money into action when you have the edge. Playing multiple hands will increase the fluctuation of your bankroll. To decrease this fluctuation, you must cut back on the size of your high bet. If you play 2 hands, both hands together should equal about 1½ times your standard high bet.

Example: if your standard high bet is $100, then play two hands of $75 each. Do not play more than two simultaneous hands unless you believe it is the last round of the shoe, and you also believe the advantage is high enough to justify the extra bets. In *Professional Blackjack,* Stanford Wong provides a detailed explanation of the simultaneous-hand logic. All serious players should have this book, and study it. Casual players should accept the above two-hand maximum recommendation as fact.

KELLY BETTING

Now we are getting into advanced betting methods for players who use true edge estimations. The recommendations above with regards to estimating your high bet as a fixed proportion of your bankroll, based on the number of decks in play, are not hard and fast rules for players who can bet more accurately according to their actual advantage on any given hand.

To oversimplify it somewhat, "Kelly" betting is attempting to bet a proportion of your bankroll equal to your advantage over the house. I.e., with a 1 percent edge, you would bet 1 percent of your bankroll. Theoretically, this is the fastest way to increase the size of your bankroll. Practically, it's impossible to follow such a betting scheme strictly. Any player who is using a true count system, however, should *always* follow conservative Kelly betting principles. The main reason for using a balanced counting system is that you may size your bets properly according to your advantage. Because all "true" count methods are approximate, any attempt to follow a strict Kelly betting system is futile. Many professional use half-Kelly betting schemes, i.e., betting ½ percent of their bankroll for every 1 percent advantage. Well-financed teams often bet quarter-Kelly units or smaller.

With a traditional true count system, you'll usually find complicated charts and tables that tell you how many units to bet at each true count, according to the various game conditions, etc. With the true edge method, you don't need any charts.

I suggest the following simplified half-Kelly approach:

1. Divide your total bankroll by 400 to determine the size of one Kelly unit. With a $10,000 bankroll:

$$\text{Kelly Unit} = \$10{,}000 \, / \, 400 = \$25$$

2. Bet one Kelly unit for every ½ percent advantage you have over the house.

That's it. If you have a $10,000 bankroll, and you estimate your advantage over the house to be 1½ percent, bet $75. If your advantage is 3 percent, bet $150. Note that with the Hi-Lo Lite or Zen, you must subtract the house advantage off the top from the true edge to arrive at your advantage. With the Advanced Red Seven, you add your pivot advantage to the true edge to get your advantage. Other than that, it's pretty straightforward.

A Kelly bettor will place more money on the table than a player who bets according to a set "high bet," as recommended earlier in this chapter. The Kelly bettor will increase the size of his bankroll faster if he reassesses his bankroll size often and adjust his Kelly unit accordingly. Your fluctuation using a Kelly betting system will be much greater than your fluctuation using the standard high-bet betting system. If you have difficulty monitoring your bankroll, especially during losing streaks, then you should use a more conservative Kelly approach. Bet one-third Kelly or one-quarter Kelly.

Kelly bettors should follow the same guidelines for playing simultaneous hands as other bettors. If you play two simultaneous hands, both bets together should equal only 1½ times your optimal Kelly bet.

If you play well, in favorable games, according to the guidelines of this chapter, and if you always reassess your bankroll after winning or losing 10 high bets, you will never lose all your money. You may lose enough of your money due to normal fluctuation that you can no longer afford to play at a level you feel is worth your time and effort. But skill and persistence usually pay off for talented card counters. Remember the Profit Formula from Chapter 5. If you persist in playing with an advantage over the house, in the long run, you'll get the best of them.

Can you make it into the long run? That's the subject of the next five chapters. . . .

♠ ♣ ♥ ♦

11

THE UNENCOUNTERED COUNTER

A master of any martial art does not conquer his opponent; he allows his opponent to conquer himself. The opponent's strengths are turned against the opponent's weaknesses. The opponent loses the battle because he is fighting himself. The master wins not because he is physically stronger, but because he is mentally a step ahead of his opponent. The master is an invisible catalyst. The opponent never sees his downfall coming. His own strength and momentum are hurling him to the ground while he is busy watching out for the master's attack.

Playing blackjack for profit is a similar situation. Your opponent, the casino, has vast strength in the form of an incredibly large bankroll. Furthermore, the house sets all the rules of the "fight" and may eliminate any opponent it considers a worthy challenger. This is a tough setup. Not only do you have to play very well in order to win, but if you look like you play well, you may not be allowed to play at all.

The major weakness of the casinos is that their advantage over the player is volatile. Sometimes they have a large advantage, but at other times, they are at a disadvantage to the knowledgeable player.

In the same way that a martial arts master does not depend on his muscles to win a fight, a master of blackjack does not depend on some incredibly difficult, higher level, multi-parameter counting system to win money at the tables. Rather, he allows the volatility of the game to put money into his pockets at its own rate. He remains invisible as a counter because he is not exploiting his own strengths as much as he is exploiting the casino's weaknesses.

Single-deck games are volatile. The change in advantage is fast and great. Multi-deck games are less volatile. The change in the advantage is slow. The master counter employs a different strategy for each game, designed to disguise his counting strategy, while at the same time maximizing his win rate. These are some of his strategies:

DEPTH-CHARGING: A SINGLE-DECK STRATEGY

Casinos primarily identify counters by watching for bet variation. If you don't bet like a counter, you will not usually be considered a counter, regardless of how accurately you might be playing your cards. It is very easy for a counter catcher to count down a deck from behind or above you, using any card counting system, while monitoring your bet size. Regardless of what counting system you are using, your bet sizing will give you away. A Red Seven player would raise and lower his bets similarly to a Zen Count player. A counter using any other valid counting system would have no difficulty detecting the conspicuous betting patterns of either player.

Most camouflage techniques employed by counters are methods of disguising bet variation. Such techniques inevitably hurt your potential win rate, but without camouflage you will be frequently shuffled up on, and probably barred if you play for high stakes.

Depth-charging is a single-deck strategy which allows you to play a winning game without using a betting spread based on your count. This strategy is not recommended for Red Seven players. To take advantage of depth-charging gains, you want a system that is strong on playing strategy.

Single-deck games can be beaten with a flat bet. Unfortunately, to do so, you need a deep shuffle point. Deep penetration is hard to come by in one-deck games these days, because the casinos know that counters can beat them easily.

One type of game that often has a deep shuffle point is the full table game, when two rounds are dealt. These games are rare in Las Vegas, but still fairly common in Northern Nevada (Reno and Tahoe). The problem with these games is that they are always dealt face down, and some players hide their cards. The deep shuffle point is worthless if you cannot see the other players' cards prior to making your decisions.

If you can see the other players cards, however, this type of game can be very valuable. Let's look at how valuable.

If I set up a seven-player table, with two rounds between shuffles, and I allow the third-base player, who is using the Zen

Count, to see all of the cards of the players who play their hands before him, with a flat bet, he will win at the rate of 0.77 percent. This is with Reno rules, which allow doubling on 10 and 11 only, and the dealer hits soft 17. With downtown Las Vegas rules, where you can double on any two cards, but the dealer still hits soft 17, the flat-betting third base player will win at the rate of 1.06 percent (assuming he can see all of the other players' cards).

This player can do quite a bit better than this if he uses a conservative count strategy. For instance, if he were to always come off the top with a 2-unit bet, and only lower it to 1 unit on the second round if the count goes negative, his Reno win rate would be 0.92 percent, and in downtown Vegas, 1.23 percent.

With a more aggressive 1-to-2 betting spread, where he came off the top with one unit, then raised to 2 units on any plus count, his Reno expectation would go up to 1.31 percent, and in downtown Vegas, 1.60 percent. All of this data was obtained from running simulations of 10 million hands each with John Imming's *Universal Blackjack Engine*. Here is the data in chart form:

Zen Count, Third Base, Full Table, 10 Million Hands Each

	Flat Bet	1-2 (2 off top)	1-2(1 off top)
Reno:	0.77%	0.92%	1.31%
DT Vegas:	1.06%	1.23%	1.60%

Naturally, if you could find better rules than these, the expectations would be even higher from these same ultraconservative betting strategies. Note also that this approach is weak from the first base position. Seeing just four fewer cards per round prior to making his decisions, the first base player's win rates for these betting schemes is barely half that of the third base player.

The problem, however, for that third base player, is in seeing all of the other players' cards. There are various ways of going about this, limited only by your own creativity.

One, you could be very friendly at a table full of friendly players, and simply get them all to show you their hands as they play. Many players do not try to hide their hands from other players, so this is not necessarily all that difficult for a gregarious sort who likes talking, and who chooses his tables wisely.

Two, you could play with friends or other counters who would all show their hands to each other. Since many players already do this at blackjack tables, it need not look suspicious.

Three, you could play with one or two friends who would be positioned at the table so that they could see the cards of the players that you couldn't see. They do not need to provide you with the actual cards they see, just the change in the count. Such information could easily be passed via simple signals. Since players are allowed to see each others' cards, it would be perfectly legal.

Four, a nonplayer who is accompanying you at the table might, from a standing position, be better able to view the cards of players' hands that were hidden from you.

Perhaps you can think of more variations on this theme.

Definition: "Depth-charging" is using the depth of the deal as the primary method of gaining a long-run advantage, rather than relying on a betting spread based on card counting information. Since casinos often recognize the traditional betting strategies of card counters, the depth-charger employs a betting strategy which is not based on his count. His playing strategy is so much more effective deep in the deck that he obtains a significant edge over the house.

With a multiple-player approach, camouflage may be provided by haphazardly sizing bets on the first base side of the table. Some of the spots on the first base side may also be played using useless progression systems, with sizably smaller bets than those being placed on the third base side.

A husband/wife team wrote to me that they used this method of play successfully in a unique partnership approach. The wife sat to the right of the husband and played 3 spots with low bets. On every hand, she consulted her husband on how to play. In fact, she did not know basic strategy. The husband sometimes gave her correct advice, sometimes less than correct — which made him appear like a showoff. He, meanwhile, played either one or two spots on the third base side of the table, at substantially higher stakes than his wife. He always played his own hands according to the correct count strategy.

When depth-charging, you must be careful not to act overly interested in other players' hands, since this may look suspicious. Your primary camouflage, however, which is not betting according to the count, should be highly effective in protecting you from suspicion of counting.

Note: The value of depth-charging comes from accurately playing your cards at deep shuffle points. If you do not accurately employ strategy tables to alter your play according to the count, flat-bet depth-charging is worthless. Likewise, you will realize significant gains at deep shuffle points by knowing some of the less used strategy indices. I would advise depth-chargers to learn the more extensive Zen Count strategy tables provided in the Appendix. It is important that you realize that your gain comes from seeing and using as much card information as you can get before playing your hand. Simply sitting at a full table without getting the necessary information on the other players' down cards is not advantageous.

ONE-DECK WONGING

One of my favorite methods of depth-charging in Reno and Tahoe used to be to "Wong it" in crowded single-deck games, i.e., tablehopping and playing only when the count is favorable. This is a depth-charging strategy which can be employed by both Red Seven Count players and Zen Count players. This strategy is primarily for small stakes players.

In the big casinos, I've had no trouble getting away with this strategy making single quarter ($25) bets. I've also done it with no heat betting single $20 bills. This style of play also works best when there are other big bettors at the table. If you bet a single quarter on a table where other players are betting multiple greens and blacks, no dealer will shuffle on you, nor will you get a second glance from the pit. If you jump around betting quarters where everyone else is betting nickels (or silver!), you are more likely to raise suspicions. Do not expect to get away with this strategy with black ($100) chips or stacks of quarters anywhere.

Playing a single hand, I was able to get an average of 38 hands per hour, tablehopping crowded single-deck games, and my average edge was about 3 percent. I also tried playing 1 to 3 hands depending on how many spots I could grab, according to the number of players at the table and their positions. In this manner, I got about 70 hands per hour, with an estimated edge of about 2 percent. I played at tables where at least 3 other players were playing, and usually there were 4 or 5 other players.

One problem I encountered was not always knowing how deeply into the deck the dealer had gone. Some of my bets were met with a shuffle-up, not out of dealer counter-paranoia, but because of necessity. In such cases, I played through the hands and doubled my bet size or walked on the next round, depending on the count. I never felt any heat. I did not sit down to play my hands, but stood behind the vacant seat.

Using the Red Seven Count, you should be able to get about 25 to 30 hands per hour, at an average edge of about 3 percent, by betting only at a running count of +3 or higher. Betting quarters, this is a potential $20 per hour. It may seem like a slow grind, but for players on limited funds there is a wisdom to only playing hands where you enjoy such a large edge. Your negative fluctuations will be considerably reduced. Playing 25 hands per hour with a 3 percent edge will win at the same hourly rate as playing 75 hands per hour with a 1 percent edge. After 100 hours of play with $25 bets, each approach would potentially net a win of $1,875. The player with the 3 percent edge, however, will have put one-third as much money into action as the 1 percent edge player, who is playing 3 times faster. The faster player with the smaller edge would need a bankroll almost twice as large as the slow player to cope with his more sizable dollar fluctuation.

Consider: If there are five players at a single-deck table in Reno and you count the first round cards, you will have seen approximately 33 percent of the deck. A Red Seven Count of +3 would indicate a player edge of about 2½ percent. *You will never see an edge like this after watching only one round of a 6-deck shoe game.* In single-deck games, this occurs frequently. You do not need to use extensive strategy tables if you play only in such advantageous situations.

Single-deck games should be a gravy train for knowledgeable low stakes players. Playing multiple hands, you may be able to get more than 100 hands per hour by Wonging in on any plus count in the big South Tahoe casinos. This is a lot of action with quarter chips. Using the Red Seven Count, the player edge is about 1 percent with this approach. With the Zen Count, I would estimate a 1½ percent edge. You can't estimate your edge with any kind of precision for this approach because of the varying conditions — different numbers of players at the tables, various deck depletions, betting on various numbers of simultaneous hands, etc. But low stakes players should strive to play fewer hands at higher advantages. If you are using a true edge adjustment, you may bet in half-Kelly units. Just don't try to get away with too much. I.e., if you see an edge of six percent, and in one-deckers this will happen, don't forget that this is a low stakes strategy. A $50 or $60 bet could get you booted.

OPPOSITION BETTING

Opposition betting is a multi-deck betting strategy. It is especially advisable where pit bosses are liable to be watching your betting patterns. To beat multi-deck blackjack games, you must understand what you are up against. I'll be honest with you. These games are tough to beat. Many players fail to comprehend two basic facts of the multi-deck challenge.

Fact 1: You cannot beat multi-deck games significantly with a flat bet or even a small spread, regardless of your system. To get a significant edge in a multi-deck game usually requires a spread of *1 to 8 units or more.* The only exception to this rule would be for a table-hopper who plays only when the count is favorable. In essence, this would not be flat-betting but using a spread in which the minimum bet is zero units. You should view tablehopping in this way because it is necessary to spend the time watching, counting and waiting until you can place your bets. Tablehopping is a camouflage technique which makes you appear to be a flat or small-spread bettor.

Fact 2: Multi-deck games are less vulnerable to traditional count strategies because the shifts in advantage are less volatile. Many players fail to grasp this because they do not understand how card counting works. This is an actual letter I received from a player many years ago:

> *"On my recent trip to Vegas I played exclusively in 4-deck games. I prefer the 4-deck games because the count doesn't jump around so much. When a shoe goes hot, it often stays that way for a long time, so I can continue to bet high for many hands in a row. In single-deck, it seems like I'll get one or two high bets then the count drops, and in no time at all they're shuffling again. In a shoe game, if the count drops real low, I leave the table and find a better game.*
>
> *"My trip was a total disaster. I couldn't have asked for better conditions, but within about 3 hours, I'd lost just about my whole playing bankroll. I was spreading quarters from one-to-four and lost $2,500. Looking back on it, the majority of my losing bets were high ($100) bets, so I guess I really only lost about 25 big bets, rather than 100 small bets. Still, I don't see how this could have*

*happened. What's worse, almost the entire loss occurred
in my last half-hour of play against the same dealer.*
*"He was dealing out about 3 decks and every shoe
the count kept climbing. By the time he'd shuffle, the running count would be between +15 and +20! Somehow, I
just kept losing. After three shoes like this, I was broke. I
use the Hi-Lo count, so I figure that by the time he shuffled, my advantage was somewhere between 7% and
10%! It seems to me the only hand I ever played at a disadvantage was the first round after the shuffle. Then the
count would go up, and it would just keep going higher.
How could I lose with such hot decks?"*

This player has one glaring misconception about how card
counting works. The reason that you bet bigger when the count is
high is because your count indicates that the remaining cards
contain a disproportionate number of tens and aces. You place a
big bet because the odds are in your favor that these high cards
will be dealt. As these cards come out of the deck, you make your
money. You will be dealt more naturals. Your doubling down
and pair splitting will pay off more. The dealer will bust his stiffs
more frequently. You are not betting big simply because the
count is high. You are betting big *because the count should come
down.*

If the count does not come down then this must mean that
those excess high cards in the deck did not, in fact, come out. If
the count continues to climb, then not only are the excess high
cards not being dealt, but a disproportionate number of low cards
continue to be dealt, much to your disadvantage.

If the dealer shuffles when the count is +15 to +20, then this
means that all of those high cards are clumped together in the undealt portion of the shoe. If this happened three shoes in a row,
then contrary to what this player's count indicated, he never
played with an advantage over the house. When the count stays
high, your high bets are all for naught.

When your count goes up in a single-deck game, it is far
more likely to come down than in a multi-deck game. It is this
volatility that makes the one-deck games so profitable. Ideally,
you make small bets while the count is rising, and large bets as it
comes back down.

Had this player been in a shoe game in which the count kept
going down to about -15 to -20 prior to every shuffle, then more

than likely, ironic as it may seem, this player probably would have won more money than he would have lost, since this situation would indicate that all the excess low cards were clumped in the undealt portion of the shoe. Such a clumpings of cards often occur purely through chance. If the dealer were purposely clumping high cards, then cutting them out of play through sleight of hand, this would be cheating.

Definition: opposition betting is sizing your bets so as to appear to be raising your bets when the count is going down and lowering your bets when the count is going up. The purpose of opposition betting is to get a large spread. The following is an explanation of how one Vegas pro gets away with it; I've paraphrased his words and changed enough details to protect his identity:

"I've been playing blackjack for thirty years. For about the first twenty, I didn't know anything about counting. At one point, I tried to read Thorp's book but the system was beyond me. Revere's book became my bible because his point count system was powerful and so much easier. I still use it. By the time I'd started counting, I was well known in the casinos as a high roller. I was comped most everywhere and still am. My basic method of camouflage, once I'd started counting, was simply to keep playing as much as possible the way I'd always played.

"I buy in at the craps table and usually spend my first ten or fifteen minutes playing craps for nickels. I'll often get a whole rack of chips — half quarters, half nickels. I never hide chips, or pocket chips, or try to look like I'm losing. I never did that before I was a counter, so why should I start now? Whether you're counting or not, sometimes you win, sometimes you lose. When I lose a lot, I sulk around. I make a lot of noise about it when I win big. The only time I pocket chips is when I cash out. I'll go south with one or two blacks, and play them or cash them out later.

"When I hit the blackjack tables, I start betting with nickels — two or three at a time. If the count starts going down, I'll bet even bigger — four or five nickels. If it keeps going down, I might push six to eight of them out there. As the count goes up, I use the reverse strategy. I'll go down to a single nickel and keep betting this way until

my true count is up around +6. Sometimes I'll go through a couple of shoes till I get a count like this. Sometimes it happens right away. But when it does go up that high, I'll raise my bet from a single nickel to a stack of quarters in one jump. I'll just throw eight of 'em on the table like that. By this time, I'm already pegged as a non-counter because of all my stupid bets before. And if they don't have me pegged this way, they will soon. My strategy with the quarters is pretty much the same as my nickel strategy. If the count goes up, I just let my stack of quarters ride. While the count is this high, I make sure I've got a couple hundred bucks on the table. It's important to me not to raise my bet if the count goes up even higher. You see, I start raising it when the count's coming back down. Dealers always change colors on you when you bet stacks of chips. If I win with eight quarters, he'll pay me off with a couple of blacks. The next stack of chips I push out there will have those blacks on the bottom. They think they're jacking up my bets by coloring me up! By the time my true count is down to +3 or so, I'll be making bets of $500 to $600. I'd say my average bet is about $250 to $350. My average low bet is probably about $15 to $20.

"About the only time I might be suspected of counting is when I make my jump from a nickel to a couple hundred bucks. Before and after that, I usually raise and lower my bets in reverse.

" A lot of times I'll jump my bets around according to whether I'm winning or losing. Often, I mix up my colors and have reds, greens and black in the same stack. It drives dealers nuts. Part of my method is to look like I just don't have much of a method. Sometimes I bet high off the top of the shoe. For the most part, I play nickels with low counts and greens and blacks with high counts. When I make my big jump, I wait until the time seems right for it. If the count is high and I've only got a nickel riding on the bet, I'm likely to split fours or fives, or maybe stand on a twelve against a ten. After a play like that, dealers love to see you start playing with real money. You see, they know I've got the greens and blacks. I'm sitting there with half a rack of them in front of me. I don't make foolish plays when I'm betting high, though.

"I've watched dozens of counters get 86'd. Most of them are young. They always spread from one to four. They're so easy to spot it's laughable. Sometimes I think my best camouflage is that I'm old and bald. My second best camouflage might be that I've got a lot of money. Counters look hungry. There's probably not much a young guy can do about this. But still, he can change his one-to-four spread to something that looks less intelligent. All the books say spread from 1 to 4 or 1 to 8. There's not a pit boss in Vegas who hasn't read most of these books. When you play like the books say, you're advertising your smarts.

"One time I was sitting with two counters for about half an hour. During the course of that half hour, I'd placed bets as low as a nickel and as high as seven or eight hundred bucks. They were both spreading quarters from one-to-four. They keep nudging each other when I'd make a stupid play. Once I insured my natural at a low count. I had two nickels on the table. Then the true count went up to about +9 or +10 real fast. I hit my four card sixteen against the dealer's five and busted. I guess these guys got brave then because both of them raised their next bets to eight chips. Frankly, I was having a hard time not laughing, myself. Their bets had been so identical since they'd sat down, they were like the Bobbsey Twins.

"The pit boss jumped in at that point. He went through the discards and politely told these two guys to hit the road. They were upset. One of them remarked that it should be illegal for casinos to only deal to stupid players. The remark was directed at me. They ended up getting barred.

"I don't want you to think I never get any heat. There are a few casinos in this town I won't set foot in. But I've got an excellent rating at most of the places that matter. You can't fool everybody . . ."

This is a crude approach to opposition betting but it illustrates the basic camouflage techniques. Without an enormous spread, such as this player employs, you could not win much money with such a drastic betting style.

The opposition bettor wins money by getting away with a large spread. Over any extended period of play, his betting looks foolish from a card counter's perspective.

Another highly effective opposition betting technique is one developed by Ralph Stricker. I think it's important to remember that there is not one method of opposition betting. It's a camouflage technique that can be used any number of ways. Stricker bases his betting approach on the fact that in multi-deck games, neither the house nor the player has any significant edge for most of the game. The player may take advantage, in the form of camouflage bet-sizing, during these long periods of play when there is no significant advantage for either side. As a counter, you can make the majority of your changes in bet size appear to be either haphazard or based on some non-counting progression-type system. Stricker reports that he and his students have had phenomenal success in the 6-deck Atlantic City games using a progression-type system through "neutral" counts, yet actually spreading from 1 to 10 when the edge was significant one way or the other.

To test the feasibility of this approach in Nevada, I tried my own method, using the Zen Count. At all negative counts, I bet one nickel. Any time my advantage was between -½ percent to +½ percent, I alternated my bets. First I bet a nickel, then I bet a quarter capped with a nickel. Then a nickel, etc. I did this regardless of whether the running count was rising or falling. When my advantage was greater than +½ percent, I bet two quarters capped with a nickel.

The advantage from betting in this manner is close to what my advantage would be if I were simply and without camouflage jumping my bets from $5 to $55. Yet, when I tried this betting technique in three Vegas casinos, my high bets never raised an eyebrow. By the time I'd made my first high bet, I was halfway into the shoe and had been alternating high-low-high-low for quite a few hands. It looks like a worthless progression because it is one. When my advantage hit a full 1 percent, I followed my low $5 bet with a $55 high bet that was simply one chip higher than my normal $30 high bet. I let this bet ride until the count went down to neutral, then went back to my alternating bets.

There are as many approaches to opposition betting as there are progression type systems. I won't recommend any one approach because I feel it's important that you never look like you're playing "by the book." How much of a spread you can get with when you're using this approach is limited by your personal bankroll, the house table limits, your creativity, your guts, your act . . .

You cannot practically use opposition betting tactics in one or two-deck games. My experience with attempting it was that too often, by the time I made my camouflage bet, either the count changed too radically or the shuffle occurred. In games of four or more decks, opposition betting takes advantage of a factor that would ordinarily make counting ineffective — the slow volatility of the edge. A player with a sufficient bankroll to play house limits will often find multi-deck games more profitable than single-deck games.

One drawback to opposition betting: Your bankroll fluctuations will be sizable. It takes a healthy bankroll to use any large spread because of the size of your high bets. You cannot use opposition betting tactics with a small spread. Your camouflage bets will nullify profit potential.

Many players use the terms "hot" shoe or "cold" shoe. Too often, players misuse these slang terms because of their misunderstanding of how counting works. *Definition: a hot shoe is a shoe with a great fluctuation in advantage.* Specifically, the count goes up, then comes down, then goes up, then down, etc. A cold shoe is one with little fluctuation, regardless of whether the count stays neutral, continuously climbs, or steadily falls through the shoe. A continuously falling count could be advantageous since so many high cards are being dealt, but you will realize small profits from such shoes. Your bet size will likely be small, and you will be playing your hands as if the count were low. Most shoes are neither cold nor hot, but somewhere between cool and lukewarm. This is where opposition betting shows its power.

Opposition betting in multi-deck games is similar to depth-charging in single-deck games. What you are doing is invisibly turning the volatility of the edge to your favor. Since the volatility is diminished in multi-deck games, it's necessary to use a large spread. But the slow volatility allows you increased camouflage betting tactics. Keep in mind that the more camouflage you use, the more you will actually hurt your win rate. For this reason, the Stricker approach strikes me as the most advantageous. Bet one unit when the house has the edge. Use a stupid progression when the edge is about neutral. And bet whatever your bankroll can afford when you have the edge. The slow volatility of the game makes possible all the camouflage you need. Try opposition betting and you'll realize immediately why it works. For most of my play, if I were sitting next to a player who was using my betting approach, I would not guess him to be a counter. Neither will the casinos. It would often require hours of personal observation to identify an opposition bettor with any degree of certainty. For this reason, opposition betting is one of the best approaches to games where a large spread is necessary to obtain a significant edge over the house.

High stakes opposition bettors tell me that the best progression-type systems to use for camouflage purposes are the typical gamblers' progressions. Either parlay your wins by adding chips, doubling up, etc., or chase your losses in a similarly predictable fashion, throughout neutral portions of the shoe.

With a moderate 1-to-4 spread, a 6-deck game is not worth much more than about 0.2 percent to a card counter who sits through the negative shoes. If you quit the table at negative counts, an opposition bet-jumping 1-to-10 spread will make this game worth about 0.6 percent. If you make it a practice to seek out games with shuffle points of between one and one-and-one-half decks, you should be able to get close to a 1 percent edge in 6-deck games using this betting style. You'll look less like a counter. You'll significantly raise your expected return. If you get your spread by lowering your low bet rather than raising your high bet, you'll also be able to decrease your bankroll fluctuations.

For instance, if you currently spread from $25 to $100, try opposition betting with a spread from $5 to $100. Perhaps bet a nickel on low negative counts; use a haphazard $10 to $50 on relatively "neutral" counts. And jump to $100 on high counts. Not only would you triple your potential win rate, you'd noticeably cut your bankroll fluctuations. Using such a large spread is similar to tablehopping in that the vast majority of your serious money bets are at high counts.

In a nutshell:

1. In multi-deck games, almost half of your hands are played when neither you nor the dealer has any significant edge.

2. During these "neutral" hands, a good card counter would break even if he were flat-betting.

3. Betting progression type systems are not detrimental to your advantage, they are merely worthless, i.e., they will not affect your basically break-even game one way or the other.

4. During these neutral hands, therefore, you may bet like a complete fool in order to establish this image for the dealer, pit boss, etc. This will increase your bankroll fluctuations, so you do not want to place your highest bets in neutral portions of the shoe. You just want to alter your bet continually with no count justification.

5. Card counters are generally suspected and identified by their betting styles, not how they play their hands. Don't overdo "stupid" camouflage plays. Most of the time, you will not need such plays to camouflage your counting. Your seemingly foolish betting is your best camouflage.

To return to the analogy of the martial arts master: The master continually signals false attacks on his opponent, attacks which are never launched; he is merely waiting for his opponent to be off balance. The opponent gains much confidence during the master's waiting period because the master's false attacks are so impotent. When the opponent loses his balance, as he will, even his perspective is unstable. He does not see the actual attack of the master.

And isn't this how a pool hustler works? And a professional poker player? And a chess master? Card counting is a science. Beating the casinos at blackjack is an art.

12

IDIOT CAMOUFLAGE

Camouflage is a military term that means disguise, deception, or pretense. A soldier has a better chance at survival if he looks like the rest of the jungle. For a card counter, camouflage means essentially the same thing. It's an act that pegs you as Ted Tourist or Harry Highroller or Donald Drunk — anyone but Clyde Counter.

There are many aspects to camouflage. In Chapters Ten and Eleven, various types of betting camouflage were described. There is also *dramatic camouflage* that most successful players find to be as important as card counting when it comes to being a consistent winner. Dramatic camouflage would include such subtle touches as appearing uninterested in other players' cards, or being preoccupied with idle table chatter. It would include the ability to raise bets as if chasing losses, or as if you believe you are on a winning streak. This dramatic camouflage is one of the most difficult aspects of card counting for a player to learn. Some people are born actors; most people are not. Show me a successful card counter and I'll show you a person who has all the innate abilities of the con artist.

One type of camouflage which many players use, often because they lack the subtle skills of the dramatic camouflage expert, is *idiot camouflage.*

As you might suspect, idiot camouflage is simply making an obviously stupid play. If the pit boss starts watching you suspiciously, you can play like an idiot. You split a pair of sixes against a dealer's ace, then you stand on your soft total of 14 (versus anything!). This, of course, looks so idiotic that the pit boss soon turns away. Now you can do whatever you want for the next hour and get rich.

Or, at least, that's the way idiot camouflage is supposed to work. Unfortunately, what usually happens is that ten minutes later, the new floorman comes by, or the dealers change, or you start to wonder about the eye upstairs, so you have to make another idiot play or two.

If you have not been blessed with acting talents, you may tend to overcompensate for this drawback by sprinkling your play with substantial amounts of idiot camouflage. Idiot camouflage has one thing in its favor: *it's easy*. It has one thing going against it: *it's costly*.

The counter's edge is small. It doesn't take many stupid plays to wipe out your profit potential. If you're not a born actor, and you feel that idiot camouflage is what keeps you in the game, here are two rules to remember:

1. Reserve your stupid plays for your smallest bets.

If you've got big money on the table, this is the wrong time to try to look dumb. If you're using a 1-to-8 spread, the same stupid play could cost you eight times more money when you have a high bet out.

2. Use a stupid play only when it is necessary.

Don't try to prove to every dealer you sit down against that you're no threat. Most dealers don't pay attention to how you're playing. They watch players all day long and they're bored stiff with the game. Try to make small talk if you can.

Two-Bit Deceptions

There are some errors that cost a lot, but others that cost little. I call the cheap ones "two-bit deceptions," because they all cost about 25¢ or less for every ten bucks you have bet on your hand. For big players, this could mean a couple bucks for every black chip, but if your expectation is a few hundred bucks per hour, you may find occasional value in giving up a few bucks for camouflage. My source for the cost of these plays is once more, the card counter's bible, Don Schlesinger's *Blackjack Attack*.

Hit/Stand Camouflage

Most of your decisions are hit/stand decisions, so misplays on these hands can be costly. One great device that multi-deck tablehoppers can use is to always stand on hard 16 vs. 10. Since you're tablehopping to avoid negative counts, you'll only misplay this hand when it's a borderline decision anyway. This is one of the hands that casinos watch to see if players vary their decisions. So, don't vary. You could even announce that you always hit this hand, which is improper basic strategy, and then follow through with your seemingly stupid strategy. This hand also occurs frequently enough that they're bound to notice your consistent erroneous play. But don't try this ploy if you're not a tablehopper. It will cost you too much.

Another stand decision you might always play wrong, without much of a loss, occurs when you have a pair of sevens versus a dealer ten in a single-deck game. This is, of course, that one weird total of 14 where the correct basic strategy is to stand rather than hit. Unfortunately, just about every blackjack book (other than this one!) since Thorp's *Beat the Dealer* has explained this in detail. It's a play that smart players make, and many pit personnel know it. It's actually a borderline basic strategy play. You won't lose much by hitting your 7-7 v. 10.

A few other cheap hit/stand mistakes: hitting a total of 12 vs. 4, 5 or 6, and hitting 13 vs. 2 or 3, all look pretty dumb, but don't cost much at neutral counts. In fact, you'll note that your Hi-Lo Lite chart indicates that you stand on all of these hands at a count of 0 or above.

Any time you are close to the index number for altering your play, the cost of misplaying the hand will be small. For instance, it would look pretty stupid to stand on a 16 vs. 7, and this would be a very costly error for a non-counter. But your Hi-Lo Lite index is +4, and if your count indicates that you are +3 or more, the misplay may be wrong, but it will not be that expensive.

Always remember the two camouflage rules we began with: The bigger your bet, the more it will cost you; and don't make a foolish play unless you think it is *necessary*.

DOUBLE-DOWN CAMOUFLAGE

In general, don't make stupid double-down decisions, because twice the money is involved. If you hit your 11 against a dealer 5 instead of doubling down, the dealer could care less, and you just blew a good chance to make some money. Most tourists double down on 11. Doubling down on soft totals like A-2, A-3, A-4, or A-5, used to peg a player as a card counter. So, many counters avoided these basic strategy plays. These days, with so many casinos selling accurate basic strategy charts in their gift shops, it doesn't mean much anymore to play these hands correctly. There are a few two-bit double-down errors that you can make at neutral counts. It doesn't cost much to double down on your 10 vs. 10, your 11 vs. A, or your total of 8 vs. 6. All of these plays look much dumber than they are.

PAIR-SPLIT CAMOUFLAGE

Don't make stupid pair-split decisions. You're doubling your money on the table when most dealers don't know correct pair-splitting basic strategy anyway. One exception: occasionally, you'll have a very high count and a pair of tens vs. a dealer low card. Your count may indicate that you should split the tens. There are some Indian reservation casinos, riverboat casinos, and foreign casinos where most people play so stupidly that you can go right ahead and split those tens and just blend into the crowd. But in Nevada, and many major casinos anywhere, this is one pair split hand you ought to play incorrectly. Likewise, it is one of the few hands you ought to play incorrectly when you have a high bet on the table. Splitting ten-valued cards is an unusual play for both stupid and smart players. Few players break up a hand totaling 20. This play often raise suspicions because it is only made by rank beginners and card counters. If you've been playing an otherwise intelligent game, you probably won't pass for a rank beginner.

There are a few pair-split basic strategy violations that fall into the category of two-bit deceptions. Some of these plays look pretty stupid. With a neutral count, failing to split a pair of nines versus a deuce costs little, and looks very amateurish. This is one of those errors tourists always make because they don't want to break up an eighteen. Better yet, and it costs just a bit more, splitting 9s against an ace looks really dumb.

A couple plays that really do cost almost nothing (about 1¢ per $100 bet), and look far stupider than they are: hit a pair of 2s or 3s versus a dealer 4, instead of splitting.

INSURANCE CAMOUFLAGE

As for insurance, casinos like to tell players one important rules: *always take even money*, i.e., insure every natural; it's the only bet on the table you can't lose. Players who do not always insure their naturals are highly suspect. Showing any sign of in-

Two-Bit Deceptions
Cost per $10 Bet / Neutral Count

Stand 12 v. 3	20¢	Double 11 v. A	20¢
Stand 16 v. X	8¢	Double 10 v. X	20¢
Hit 12 v. 4	6¢	Double 8 v. 6	20¢
Hit 12 v. 5	30¢	Hit 2,2 v. 4	1¢
Hit 12 v. 6	20¢	Hit 3,3 v. 4	1¢
Hit 13 v. 2	20¢	Stand 9,9 v. 2	20¢
Hit 13 v. 3	40¢	Split 9,9 v. A	40¢

telligence at a blackjack table can be dangerous. Actually, it's not all that expensive to always insure your naturals. If you were flat-betting $100 per hand, it would only cost you about $1.35 per 100 hands. That's pretty cheap camouflage for a black chip bettor. Ironically, it actually costs card counters less than one hundredth of a percent of their action to always insure their naturals. This is because counters bet more at higher counts, when it is not only correct to insure naturals, but more naturals occur. The best way to insure your naturals is to quickly yell out, "Even money!" Do this before you've even had a chance to look at the other cards on the table. If you're playing multiple hands, take even money for your natural, but don't insure your other hands! This always looks great. (Of course, if the count justifies it, you do want to insure the other hands, but don't insure them if it's just a borderline justification.)

Other than for this even money play, don't make stupid insurance plays. Follow your count.

I am of the opinion that small stakes card counters should *never make any idiot camouflage plays.* Likewise for most hit-and-run counters, who get in and out of games, pits, and casinos quickly. If you don't get rated, don't get a VIP card, and don't give your name, you don't need camouflage; you need Reeboks.

Idiot camouflage is primarily for high stakes players who are going for the comps as well as the money. Even these players must remember that *there's no real difference between a player who uses constant idiot camouflage and a real idiot.*

♠ ♣ ♥ ♦

13

High Rollers Survival Guide

This chapter is especially important for counters who play green ($25) and black ($100) action and higher. Small stakes players will find some of the information herein useful, especially the toking guidelines and the information on preferential shuffles, but some of the other concerns addressed will have little applicability to low stakes play. *Big players need all of this information to ensure their survival.*

You Don't Know Me

Card counters must be very careful of their associations with other card counters in the casinos. It is not wise to socialize in the casinos with other card counters. Even if you are traveling with a fellow player, in the pits, you should be strangers.

If one of you is identified as a card counter, you do not want suspicions cast upon the other. Many big money players even avoid associations with other counters in the casino restaurants and other public areas. Pit bosses and hosts, as well as other floor and surveillance personnel eat in the casino restaurants and buy magazines in the gift shops. You never know whom you'll run into, or where.

Don't take unnecessary chances.

House Phone Hang-Ups

Although most counters feel that the casino hotel room phones are unlikely to be bugged by the casinos, as this would constitute a federal crime, many still feel it is unsafe to call other counters room-to-room within the same casino. The worry is not that the private conversation may be monitored, but that there may be an electronic record of the room-to-room phone connections.

If the player in Room 206 is identified as a card counter, could surveillance get access to a record which would show that during the weekend Room 206 connected via his room phone half a dozen times to the guest in room 308? Does this sound overly paranoid? There are teams of players who believe they have been identified by this method.

The solution? Leave your room and call your friends via any white courtesy phone, many of which are located throughout the casino. Naturally, if you're the paranoid type, and you believe all casino phones are bugged, FCC regulations be damned, then you'll just have to call from pay phones and speak in a code that only you and your friends understand.

SHIFT CHANGE VANISHING ACT

All 24-hour casinos have three work shifts — day, swing, and grave. The hours of each shift may vary somewhat. Day is from about 10 AM to 6 PM; swing is from 6 PM to 2 AM; grave is from 2 AM to 10 AM. When you first sit down to play, if you intend to play for any length of time, ask the dealer how long until she gets off, or if she just started, or whatever, depending on the time of day. This must be small talk, mixed in with how's the weather been, and are you beating everybody today? What you really want to know is when the shift change is, and if the bosses change at the same time the dealers do, and if the change is "staggered" over a period of time, etc. Once you learn this information, you should keep a record of it, so that whenever you return to that casino you do not have to go through this process again.

The reason you want this information is that *you do not want to play through a shift change.* Whether you are winning or losing, and regardless of whether you think you may be suspected of skillful play, playing through a shift change is generally a bad idea. You just don't want the swing boss discussing your play with the grave boss. Let the grave boss form his own opinion.

If you intend to play a few more hours that day, the shift change is an excellent time to take a break, grab a snack, take a shower, and come back in forty-five minutes a new man or woman. If a shift change suddenly takes you by surprise, you look up and new suits are standing around gabbing with the old suits, you blew it. But remember what time it is, and if you add and subtract eight hours, you'll know when all the shift changes occur in this casino. Next time, you'll be long gone for the changing of the guard.

TOKING GUIDELINES

"Toking" is casino slang for tipping. Some card counters believe their tokes can used to obtain more advantageous conditions. Often, they are wrong. Let's examine the value of tokes to a card counter. All tokes maybe categorized as either *general* or *specific.*

GENERAL TOKES

A general toke is a toke made to maintain or improve the player's long-run playing conditions. Placing a bet for the dealer shortly after beginning play, in the hopes of favorably influencing the dealer, is an example of a general toke. This dealer may be less suspicious, more apt to deal deeper into the deck, and more likely to ignore a betting spread. Tips made solely for the purpose of camouflage, in order to give the appearance of a high roller, would also fall into the category of general tokes. This type of tipping is recommended by Ian Andersen in *Turning the Table on Las Vegas.*

To avoid excessive general toking, a player must realistically consider his expected average hourly profit, based on hands per hour, average bet size, and approximate advantage over the house. The expected hourly win is estimated by using the Profit Formula from Chapter Five. Example: An average bet of $50, at 120 hands per hour, with a long-run advantage over the house of one percent from card counting:

Expected hourly win = $50 x 120 x .01 = $60.

From this expectation, the player may decide how much he wishes to "give back" to the dealer in tokes. A frequent error of rookie card counters is to toke excessively.

Many times I have seen a player betting quarters, using a moderate spread, and playing a solid game, suddenly toss a $25 chip to the dealer because the player had a lucky 20-minute run and won a few hundred dollars. Paying a dealer so lavishly for a winning streak is a sure road to the poor house. Winning streaks occur frequently, and to toke after every one is expensive. Losing streaks occur just as frequently, though I have yet to see a dealer toke a player who has just lost a few hundred dollars. Toking after a win should be classified as a general toke. The size and frequency of such tokes should be calculated according to long-run expectations.

Let's assume the player enjoys a long-run advantage of one percent over the house, with an average bet size of $100. At a full table, this player's expectation is not more than $60-70 per hour. A $25 toke in this game represents a sizable portion of this player's hourly expectation.

Consider a casino with crowded six-deck games, where a table-hopper with a moderate betting spread enjoys an advantage of about one percent. If this player is making $25 average bets, he would be unwise to toke at all under such conditions, as his expected rate of profit would only be about $15 per hour.

You must be realistic in estimating your hourly win rate. It would be wise to estimate total toke-dollars as a per-hour average, based on how much of your potential win you feel should be reinvested, either for camouflage purposes or otherwise. Tips to cocktail waitresses and any other expenses incurred in casino play should also be considered from this perspective.

SPECIFIC TOKES

Specific toking is toking for *an immediate potential gain.* Toking a dealer in an effort to influence him to deal one more round before shuffling at a high count is a specific toke. The size of the toke must be determined on the basis of the potential gain from one specific hand. The player advantage from card counting rarely exceeds 3 percent on a high count, and in most multi-deck games, an advantage over 2 percent is uncommon. Players who make specific tokes should closely monitor results. How often does a bet placed for a dealer fail to influence his action? If a dealer does not suspect you of counting cards, he may shuffle anyway, unaware of the toke's purpose. With a 2 percent advantage, a single hand would profit you $2 for every $100 you bet. Toking the dealer $1 for every $100 bet would split the profit 50-50 between you and the dealer, but he will likely think you are a cheapskate to betting $100 and only toking him a buck. Toking the dealer $5 for a $100 bet would be paying him more than twice your expectation.

Specific toking is of no practical value to most players. General toking, as part of an act, may occasionally be useful. Such toking should be carefully planned to increase profits, not eat them. Card counters making average bets of less than $25 should not toke at all, unless, of course, you are a generous person and it makes you feel better to give money to people. Don't think of it as part of your counting strategy.

DEALERS WHO CHEAT

Cheating does exist in casinos. Unfortunately, there is little the player can do to protect himself, except walk away from any table where he suspects he is being cheated. Players who are playing for low stakes will be less likely to be cheated than high stakes players. Players in single or double-deck hand held games will be more likely to be cheated than players in shoe games.

Blackjack pros and card sharps agree that most casino blackjack dealers are honest. Blackjack pros know this because they continue to profit from high stakes card counting year after year. If cheating dealers were common, this would be impossible. Card sharps are among the few who can recognize cheating moves. Most card sharps will tell you that you have to be able to perform any of the cheating moves yourself in order to recognize them. They will also tell you that some of the most common cheating methods are not detectable by anyone.

A talented card cheat would not perform any detectable moves and would not resort to any device which could be used as evidence if discovered — such as hidden or marked cards. If he stacks the deck, performs false shuffles, peaks at the top card, or deals the second card from the top, all of these movements will appear natural. Unless you have personally witnessed close-up demonstrations of these techniques by expert card manipulators, you would be amazed at some of the "miracles" a slight-of-hand artist can perform with a standard deck of playing cards.

There are only a few basic warning signals that are easy for the player to detect in attempting to avoid cheating dealers. Probably the easiest, least detectable and most common cheating technique is simply to make incorrect payoffs. Always pay attention to the amount you have bet and the amount of your payoff. Especially, watch for incorrect payoffs on blackjacks and insurance bets. If a hand occurs where you, or the dealer, or both, take many small hit cards, be sure you add up the totals of both hands. If the dealer collects your money before you finish adding, stop him. Make sure all payoffs are correct. You'll get faster at this as you gain experience.

A false shuffle is a difficult cheating move to detect. It may be used in either single or multi-deck games. No sleight-of-hand is necessary for this move. The dealer simply locates a clump of high cards by noting their approximate position when he places them in the discard tray (or his hand, if single-deck). Then, when later shuffling the cards, he controls this clump and positions it where it will be cut out of play.

No other sleight or move is necessary. A shuffle of this type is undetectable to players, pit bosses, and the eye-in-the-sky. Yet, the dealer will completely nullify any potential gain from card counting and, over the long run, will win a greater amount of money from all the players who play against him.

This type of cheating is particularly devastating to card counters because it causes the count to continually go up as the excess low cards are dealt. The counter raises his bets, but the expected high cards never come out.

The easiest way to handle this type of cheating is to leave the table. Your only clue that this false shuffle technique is being used will be that you will notice the count is always high when the dealer shuffles. If this occurs frequently, leave the table.

In most Nevada casinos, it would be difficult for a dealer in a shoe game to steer a clump of cards anywhere in the shuffled decks, because most casinos have house shuffle routines that must be followed. Most players who have reported suspicious games to me, where the count always went up, ended high, and never came down, shoe after shoe, have experienced this disturbing phenomenon in foreign casinos. My first suspicion would not, in fact, be a false shuffle, but a "short" shoe which had aces and tens removed (and/or extra low cards added).

The second warning signal that you may be being cheated also involves a false shuffle. Again, the mechanics of the shuffle will be undetectable, but the result of the shuffle will be that the dealer will get a natural on the first hand.

There are dozens of methods a card expert could use to control just one ace and one ten to be dealt to his own hand after the shuffle, and you will not see any of them. Just remember that a dealer should get a blackjack about once out of every twenty hands. If he gets a blackjack first hand after a shuffle, it's usually just luck. The odds against him getting a natural first hand after a shuffle twice in a row are more than 400 to 1. Be suspicious. If it happens a third time in a row, the odds against it having occurred due to chance are more than 8,000 to 1. It's still probably just luck, but I'd find another dealer.

In fact, any time you feel uncomfortable about a dealer, leave the table. Don't take chances. If you think a dealer is handling the cards in an unnatural or suspicious manner, don't try to catch him in the act of cheating. You would probably be unable to spot it, and if you did, you could not prove it. Reporting suspected cheats to the casino will get you nowhere. Unless you can provide solid evidence, and you have witnesses to back you up, you will be viewed as a troublemaker, a paranoid, a sore loser, or possibly a scam artist.

Most casino blackjack dealers are honest. If you are on a losing streak, don't blame cheating dealers. If you're playing for high stakes, you would be wise to seek a demonstration, and possibly a course of instruction, from a card expert who thoroughly understands cheating moves, especially those which can be used in casino blackjack. There are also books and videotapes available on the subject. (See the Appendix for some recommended titles.) Still, don't expect to see a good cheat. I've had personal demonstrations by some of the best card sharps in the world. I've had the moves explained to me in detail and performed in slow motion. All a card sharp can teach you is how to spot a sloppy or inexperienced cheat. An expert is undetectable. In any case, unless you have proof, your best defense is to quit that table at your first suspicion.

You should avoid getting involved in "private" illegal blackjack games. If you play for high stakes, and especially if you take junkets with other high rollers, you are liable to be invited to play in private games. This is risky. I know one pro who couldn't resist such an offer. He didn't realize he was being cheated until he'd lost $15,000.

Stick to the legal casinos. You'll less likely to be cheated in a legal establishment. If you ever have even the slightest suspicion you are being cheated, quit the table. Most games are legit, but don't take chances.

Indian reservation casinos are particularly dangerous because you will not be protected by state or federal laws, only by the tribal laws of that reservation. In 1996, a California blackjack player who discovered that marked cards were in use at the Indian reservation casino where he'd lost many thousands of dollars, learned that despite the fact that the reservation acknowledged that he'd been cheated with marked cards, he could not get his money back. The state law was not applicable, and the tribal law did not require that he be paid back for his losses.

Cheating by Any Other Name

The most common form of cheating at blackjack in Nevada is "preferential shuffling." This is widely practiced at the hand-held games. It has become especially popular since the state Gaming Control Board ruled that it was legal.

It does violate the Nevada cheating statutes, but it is very difficult for a player to win a court case against a casino in Nevada, especially when the Gaming Board opposes the law as written.

Preferential shuffling is when a dealer counts cards, then shuffles up if the deck favors the player, but deals when the deck favors the house. Obviously, no card counting system can beat this house strategy, since the player will never play with an advantage. Card counters need not worry about being cheated via this method, because counters immediately recognize it.

The count goes up, the dealer shuffles. It's very obvious. The counter leaves and goes to another casino. This is actually a way that the casinos cheat non-counters who do not recognize what is happening. Some casinos use it to milk their big players. Personally, I find it despicable.

High-Tech Surveillance

Many of the techniques of betting camouflage which have been offered thus far in this book will not deceive the new high-tech surveillance computers. These computers can be used to track the count, and rate players according to their skill levels. Traditional card-counting strategies will be recognized, including just about any form of bet variation that results in the player betting more on advantageous hands, and less on hands where the house has the advantage.

This type of software allows the unseen operator to enter all players' bets and playing decisions either while play is in progress, or afterwards from the surveillance videos. The analysis feature then evaluates the skill levels of all players at the table.

The normal types of betting camouflage that card counters have traditionally used with great success will not fool the computer. Even the most radical forms of opposition betting, which will fool most pit bosses, will not fool a computer tracking program.

The best strategy for card counters is to move around frequently, changing tables often, and not playing for extended periods in the same pit. This type of tablehopping will not totally foil the computer, but it will take a very dedicated human analyst to follow your play.

Team strategies, where a big player gets called into games, plays a few hands, then moves on, also work well. Again, a dedicated human could use the software to evaluate this type of play, but it will require that every table the suspected counter enters be counted from the beginning of the shoe in order to know whether this tablehopping player is, in fact, moving into rich decks, or just moving around. There is more information on this type of play in Chapter 15.

Shuffle tracking strategies are probably the counting strategies least likely to be recognized by this type of software. The shuffle tracking analysis features are very crude, and would likely only recognize players who were using computers to track shuffles. Human shuffle trackers will not have the consistency nor the precision of play to be recognized as shuffle trackers by computer tracking programs. There is more information on shuffle tracking in Chapter 14.

Many major casinos now use this type of software, though I suspect that many of the casinos that have purchased it use it more haphazardly than universally. It is simply too time consuming to evaluate all players this way. High rollers should probably keep abreast of the Counter Surveillance Network on the Blackjack Forum Web Site, which lists the casinos which are using this type of software as well as other surveillance techniques.

Traveling With Cash

It has become quite dangerous to travel with large amounts of cash. In the U.S., many police agencies will confiscate cash as "drug money," with no questions asked. Even though you may not be in possession of any drugs, and will not be charged with any crime, current laws will not require the police to prove their accusations. Unless you can prove that the money you were carrying was not the result of illegal activities, your money will not be returned to you. Should this happen to you, you will have to hire a lawyer, and it could be expensive. It could also take many months until you get it back, if you get it back.

Traveling through airports is especially dangerous, even on domestic flights. If for some reason you match the profile of a drug courier, you may expect to have your luggage searched. One feature of that profile is that you are traveling on a *one-way ticket*. For this reason, if you will be traveling by air with cash, consider purchasing a round-trip ticket, even if you do not need the round trip. You can always cash in the return trip later. Even though you may know you are innocent, it is much cheaper and easier to avoid confiscation of your money than it is to try and get it back from the feds.

Also, wear the money on your person. Your bags are far more likely to be searched than your body. You should get a couple of money belts which you can wear inconspicuously underneath your clothing. There is nothing illegal about carrying money; it's just that the U.S. government is now allowed to relieve you of it if they have any suspicion. The only cause for suspicion they need to cite is: *you are carrying a large amount of cash.*

If you are traveling internationally, *always declare any cash you are carrying over $10,000.* If you do not declare it, and it is found, it is history. Don't attempt to hide it in your luggage or on your person. It is legal to carry cash provided you declare it. If you don't declare it, *it will be confiscated.* You will probably never get it back.

Some countries will not allow you to exit with large sums of cash in their currency, and you may find it difficult, if not impossible, to convert some currencies into U.S. dollars, or into any other easily negotiable currency. Always check local laws regarding these issues before you spend weeks hammering some casino for money you can't take with you. In most such countries, there will be black markets for currency exchange, but this could prove both dangerous and expensive.

The best way to transport large sums of money both domestically and internationally, is via American Express travelers checks. If they are confiscated at the border, no problem. American Express will replace them for full value when you report them lost. Most countries have an American Express office, where they may or may not sell you travelers checks in exchange for the local currency. This is not a paid advertisement; this is a warning.

Cash Transaction Reports

All casinos now file cash transaction reports (CTRs) on cash transactions of $10,000 or more per day. You should know that these reports are also filed by banks any time you withdraw or deposit $10K+ in a 24-hour period. This is in compliance with the U.S. Treasury Department and the IRS, who are always on the lookout for tax dodgers and money launderers. *It is very dangerous to make multiple transactions below $10K in order to avoid these reports.* The IRS calls this "structuring," and it is a crime. Even if there is no evidence that you avoided a penny of your taxes, *structuring is a crime in and of itself.*

Be careful. Try to always make your transactions in quantities of $10K or more, so that the CTRs get filed properly. Filing many CTRs will not get you into trouble unless the feds can *prove* that these CTRs are a result of illegal activities. Card counting is not a crime, but not reporting your large cash transactions is.

But, what if you don't want to give your name to the casino where you just won fifteen thousand dollars? A spokesman for the U.S. Treasury Department has stated that it would *not* be a crime for a card counter to structure casino cage deposits and withdrawals in order to avoid CTRs *for the purpose of keeping under the casino "radar,"* and possibly being identified as a card counter. After a big win, many pros choose to cash out smaller amounts over a period of time. No law has been broken, but it could be difficult to convince the IRS that this was what you were doing.

♠ ♣ ♥ ♦

14

TEAM PLAY

There is one major financial benefit from teaming up with other players. When two or more players combine their bankrolls, with the agreement that the team will share all wins and mutually absorb all losses, then each member of the team may size his bets as if the team bankroll were his personal bankroll. When more than one player works from a common bankroll, the effect on fluctuation is the same as if one player were simply playing that many more hands.

Team members should not play at the same table, unless this is necessary (such as for a depth-charging strategy). If you play at the same table, then you must all size your bets the same as if one player were playing multiple simultaneous hands. You will not reap the full benefit of your combined bankrolls.

You must trust your fellow team members, and you should all test and drill each other. Never team up with a player whose abilities or honesty you question.

ACCOUNTING

All financial considerations must be worked out, on paper, beforehand. Dividing wins and losses can be difficult when various team members contribute different amounts to the team bankroll, play various numbers of hours, and win and lose various amounts of money. To keep the bookkeeping simple, you would be wise to separate each player's contributions to the team according to investment in the team bank, hours played, and win/loss.

On one ledger, list each player's bankroll contribution. You may have a six-member team, with three members making no contribution, two members contributing $5,000 each, and one member contributing $10,000. Small teams usually judge this bankroll contribution to he worth about 50 percent of the total team win. If the team doubles their $20,000 bank, then automatically 50 percent of this win ($10,000) would be divided proportionately among the three contributors to the team bankroll. The contributor who put in twice as much money as either of the other two would take twice as much of the win.

If the team were to suffer a $10,000 loss, these three bankroll contributors would have to absorb the entire loss, in proportion to their respective contributions. It is because these team members are putting their personal money at risk that they enjoy such a sizable proportion of the win. On teams with banks in excess of $250,000, the investment share is usually more than 50 percent. There is no precise formula; each team decides what they can live with.

A second ledger is kept with the total hours played for each player. The time contribution is worth 25-50 percent of the win. If the team wins $20,000, the agreed upon proportion of this win will be divided up according to how many hours each team member played. You may have a six-member team, where one member contributes to the bankroll but does not play, while five members play various numbers of hours. In this case, only those who put in time at the tables would take a portion of this hourly payment, equal to the proportion of time each member spent at the tables.

A third ledger records the total win or loss of each player. The personal win contribution of all players is worth the remaining percentage of the total win. Players whose net results have been a loss would take none of this share. Those players who have won money for the team divide up their proportion of the total win based on their personal wins. Some teams neither reward nor penalize players for wins/losses, considering these short term results to be more due to statistical fluctuations than skill, or lack thereof. Others feel it is always good to reward winners, as this may encourage players to strive for excellence.

Larger teams often assign a win share to team management. Some may reward scouts for locating good games. Some teams pay a win percentage to analysts/programmers who devise optimal playing strategies.

It must be predetermined how expenses will be handled. Players may either agree to absorb these personally, or the team bankroll may cover all or certain specified expenses. Some teams occasionally agree to pay some players an hourly rate in addition to, or in lieu of, a win share.

Most important, it must be decided beforehand exactly how and when the team bank is to be broken. Weeks of planning can be ruined if one major bankroll contributor decides to pull out suddenly. Arguments can be avoided by settling these matters beforehand.

THE TEAM HANDBOOK

Every team, no matter what size, should develop a handbook which spells out all procedures, rules and agreements. Most new teams break up due to differences, misunderstanding, and broken verbal agreements that occur when the team suffers a major loss. Your team handbook must be a mutually agreed upon document. Any time a problem arises which is not covered in the handbook, solve it, then revise or expand the handbook to include the solution.

The areas your handbook must cover are:

1. How do players qualify for team play? What testing procedures will be used? Will only one system be allowed? How many strategy indices must be known? Will there be tests for counting speed and accuracy, true count adjustment, visual deck estimation, and shuffle-tracking talent?

2. Will the team use signals in the casino? What are the signals? Will members be tested on signals?

3. How will games be chosen for attack? Will players have any autonomy in choosing and playing games, or must all game choices be authorized by a team manager.

4. Who will act as team manager, and what will the manager's duties and responsibilities be?

5. Will there be strict guidelines on comportment and/or dress code inside the casino?

6. Who handles the trip bankroll? How is the money doled out to players? What accounting procedures will be used before and after play?

7. What betting limits are placed on players? What amount of a win or loss necessitates an immediate report to the team manager?

8. Do players toke dealers, and if so, how much, how often, and under what conditions?

9. Can team members meet in restaurants or in their rooms? Can they call room-to-room? Can team players ever bring

spouses, girlfriends, boyfriends, companions, on trips? To team meetings?

10. During playing trips, how often will team meetings be called, and who calls them?

11. If players are rewarded for hours played, are all hours booked at equal rates, or will hours be rewarded according to activity; i.e., will big players earn more per hour than spotters, etc.

12. What is the target win? Can investors add to or subtract from the team bank prior to hitting the target? Will the win be divided according to dollar investment, hours, win, duties or all of the above? How? What proportions?

13. Will violations of rules be penalized financially, and if so, how much and who determines this?

14. Will polygraph tests be used to encourage honesty? If so, who decides when this procedure will be used?

If you involve yourself in a team effort, you will discover that the more you have spelled out on paper, the smoother the team will run. You will find an excellent model for a team handbook in Don Schlesinger's *Blackjack Attack.*

In Ken Uston's books, notably *The Big Player* and *Million Dollar Blackjack,* you will find some fairly comprehensive team attack methods, including everything from bet-sizing guidelines to the precise sets of signals employed during the operations. This type of information is good to read for ideas, but it is important that you learn to develop your own methods. You always want to do some things different from what others have done. Always be ready to change those things that aren't working. Throw around ideas with your teammates. The most successful operations are those that continually change. Conditions vary so much in different casinos that you cannot always use the same modus operandi. If there was one stock team methodology, the casinos would catch onto it in no time.

EMFH TEAMS

The simplest team approach is the EMFH approach, or *Every Man for Himself.* This approach is viable with virtually any size team or bank. Because of its simplicity of execution, it's also one of the most popular team approaches.

An EMFH team is dependent on each team member being a competent card counter who is capable of beating the tables.

This type of team approach requires the highest level of trust among the participants, as it is essentially a simple agreement to share a common bankroll and all playing results.

For instance, three close friends, all of whom are card counters, might each contribute $10,000 to a common bank so that each of the three may play off of a $30,000 team bank. They need not play together, nor in the same casino(s), nor even in the same cities, nor at the same time.

Such a team might make a simple agreement to set a win target of $15,000, and to distribute profits when the target is hit, proportionately on the actual hours of play of each player. This type of agreement allows maximum flexibility for the participants. Technically, they need not ever even see each other. Actual playing times and locations will be at the convenience of the individual team members.

An EMFH team can coordinate all operations over the phone, wire-transferring funds if necessary. Such a team has no hassle of coordinating attacks on specific casinos/shifts, no possibilities of signal mix-ups, and no risk of being identified as team players with each other.

The prime requirement for this type of effort is absolute trust in each other. This type of team cannot succeed unless all members are absolutely honest with each other — re: hours of play, win/loss results, expenses, etc. There also must be a vigilant effort on the part of all team members to regularly update each other on play results, so that all are kept abreast of the actual size of the team bank.

Two Person Teams

This type of team often consists of players who play together without any attempt to disguise the fact that they are together. Since it is common for male/female couples to play together, and not uncommon for any two friends, same sex or not, to sit together and play blackjack, a two-person team does not necessarily need to hide the fact that they know each other.

There are many viable approaches for maximizing the profit potential of a two-person team. This type of team need not consist of two card counters. A single talented player can use discreet signals (verbal or nonverbal) to tell the other player how to play and bet. In the case of couples, this can usually be done quite openly, without the need for signals, as couples often help each other play their hands.

Male/female teams can also use their "couple" status simply to increase the betting spread. During uncrowded times, female companions may sit at the table without playing a hand, and this appears very natural (because it is; you see this all the time in casinos). It is also quite common for such a female companion to occasionally grab some of her husband's/boyfriend's chips and play a hand or two. This can effectively double the betting spread of a single player without appearing to.

Two person teams which consist of two talented players can also utilize their counting abilities to enhance their profits beyond what either might be able to accomplish individually. For instance, advantageous rules such as over/under (See Chapter 16), which require nontraditional counting systems, can be more effectively attacked by a two-person team in which one counts traditionally, while the other keeps the over/under count. More advanced players might also try various shuffle-tracking strategies. (See Chapter 15.)

Two person teams, because they are so often composed of close friends and/or real life couples, have a high rate of success. When two players are using a strategy, where they are playing at the same table, they also eliminate worries about win/loss reporting, as they both witness the results.

BP/SPOTTER TEAMS

Larger teams often use a *spotter* approach to team play. A spotter is a low stakes player or often a non-player who is simply watching the games, who calls in a big player (BP) via signals. Ken Uston wrote fairly extensively about this approach *(The Big Player,* 1976, and *Million Dollar Blackjack,* 1981), crediting Al Francesco with having invented it in the early 1970s.

Despite the fact that this method has been so widely publicized, it is still used successfully today. The only effective countermeasure to the BP approach is restricting mid-shoe entry. This is done in some casinos, especially in Atlantic City where they can't bar counters, but it is one of those countermeasures that costs the house dearly. The vast majority of players who want to enter mid-shoe are just regular unskilled players. And many high rollers like to change tables at whim. Restricting mid-shoe entry eliminates a lot of action from the tables, so most casinos wisely reject this countermeasure.

BP/spotter teams generally work best during crowded playing times, when lots of players are wandering around. Signals must be subtle natural gestures and easy to see. If a complex set of signals is required, much time must be spent practicing before attempting to engage such a strategy in a casino BJ pit.

I would advise any players considering a BP/spotter team approach to start small (half a dozen players at most), and allow the team to build gradually. BP/spotter approaches look great on paper, but can be quite confusing in a chaotic casino environment. When starting out, you must prearrange short sessions (not more than an hour or two), so that you may reconvene with your teammates to discuss problems, missed signals, or any aspect of the approach that seems not to be working. On your initial sessions, you may expect to be devising many new signals for previously unanticipated situations you've encountered. You must maintain flexibility to work out these details.

Because of the success of Uston's books, the casinos are well aware of this team approach, and do look out for it. Big money players who continually jump in and out of games should expect surveillance. This is one of the more difficult types of team operations to coordinate, because the combined talents of so many individuals are necessary for success. There is often a great fun factor to participating in this type of team, however, as you will continue to get together with your teammates for discussions, practice sessions and money transfers.

This team approach is one of the best ways to fool the counter-catcher software that tracks players. In order to evaluate a BP who is continually jumping in and out of shoes for short periods of play, it will be necessary for the software operator to watch videos of every shoe the BP entered, from the beginning of each deal, in order to know if the shoe was favorable when the player entered. With many tables, and videos of all of them, this could be a real headache.

Tempers can flare when a team is losing, especially if any players begin to distrust the talents or honesty of any of their teammates. A BP/spotter team operation, more than any other type of team, requires strong leadership, rigorous testing methods, and meticulous bookkeeping. With a large operation, money transfers may be frequent. All wins/losses and transactions must continually be recorded and updated. You must do this to avoid arguments about who had how much and who gave what to whom.

It is also important that all members of the team understand that *they do not know each other in the casino*. It is also unsafe to meet in the casino coffee shop or restaurants, or any public areas of the hotel/casino(s) where you are playing, as pit personnel are liable to see you together. In many casinos, it is safe to meet in one of your hotel rooms, provided you arrive separately.

THE GORILLA BP

A *gorilla BP* (another term from Uston's books) is a player who is *not* a card counter (or at least is *not* paying any attention to the cards during the play), but who makes all betting/playing decisions according to signals. The gorilla BP is often drinking heavily so that his erratic big bets appear to be more due to his Johnny Walker wisdom than anything else.

The danger of using gorilla BPs is that they often really do get drunk, and they are probably carrying a large amount of team money. What do you do if your gorilla's ability to read and follow signals diminishes dangerously? I've heard stories of such players who not only failed to heed playing/betting signals, but failed to leave the tables when given the "quit now" signal.

Another problem that sometimes arises with gorilla BPs who really do get drunk, is that even if they can accurately follow signals, they are sometimes very obnoxious, and casinos today are not as comfortable with obnoxious drunks as they used to be. If your BP is irritating other players, spilling his drink on the table or offending the cocktail waitresses, he may be asked to call it a night despite the fact that he is betting big money. Casinos are much more image conscious today.

The gorilla BP approach works best when you have a high roller who is not a card counter, and who already has a long history of big money playing with a top rating in a casino. Such a player, especially if a known loser, can often get away with murder at the tables, and the pit will usually be happy to see him winning for a change.

I would suggest using this approach with a gorilla BP who can act drunk, with a drink in his hand, but not necessarily one who is drunk. This approach should probably be avoided with a large team of spotters, as you will continually lose track of the whereabouts of your gorilla, which can be scary if he's really drunk. He might also attract thieves and pickpockets, which is another worry. He is also unlikely to know anything about his actual play results, or how much he won or lost. Gorilla BP strategies work much better with actors than with alcoholics.

THE RISK REMAINS

Other than as a consultant, I have been involved in only one team venture, in which I invested a relatively small amount, played a few hundred hours, and acted as a team manager at various times. It was a total disaster. On the very first night of play, with a dozen players, we were within $3,000 of hitting our target. Everyone was winning. We could almost taste the champagne.

The second night, we hit the negative flux, and it went downhill from there. In the first six months, with about 1000 hours of play, we lost half our bank. There were many dumb decisions that contributed to this, many having to do with expenses.

We spent $5,000 transporting more than a dozen players to a "fantastic" promotion that never happened. We spent thousands sending one player to a "great" game in Europe, where in 10 days of play, he won $600. We found some juicy games in the Southwest, and we booked hundreds of hours at these games over a period of five weeks. Unfortunately, the comps were hard to come by. Everyone required airfare, rental cars and hotel rooms. We won about $16,000, but had close to that amount in expenses. Subsequently, three players lost $26,000 on a three-week trip to various Midwestern states, with expenses of $3,000 to $4,000 to boot. The riverboat casinos were not giving out the hotel and airfare comps. A couple players who were "sure" they'd be comped by a major Atlantic City casino, had their comps rescinded when they were identified as pros. They managed to lose about $8,000, and had expenses of close to $2,000 due to coast-to-coast air travel, rental car, and hotel.

Some players who didn't really book that many hours, simply had bad losses — $8,000, $10,000, $12,000. Some players won, but not nearly enough to make up for the losses and the ridiculous expenses.

Once we had a thousand hours in on the bank, and only half our money left, it became impossible to get players to continue to play for the team. The hours would have been worthless; non-investing players just couldn't expect to make a decent hourly rate digging out a bank that was so stuck.

So, we had to start making "augment" agreements with pros who would play partially on our bank, and partially on their own. Some pros are agreeable to this type of arrangement in order to cut their personal risk. Over the next eight months, the bank slowly climbed back up. The problem with augmented play, however, was that we had originally lost the money dollar for dollar, but we were winning it back at the rate of 50¢ to 60¢ per dollar, depending on the augment. It was a long slow climb, and it was not easy to find players who wanted to augment. Most pros, if they are not connected with a team, have sufficient bankrolls to play on their own, and little desire to share profits.

Then, after having come almost all the way back to flush, over a period of six weeks, half a dozen big losses again drove the bank down to about half its starting point. Our investors, most of whom were players themselves, were asking hard questions. We started administering lie detector tests; just what we needed, more expenses!

I was calling other teams that I knew for advice, big teams with years of experience. What are we doing wrong? I started hearing all kinds of horror stories — the bank that took more than two years to break, the banks that nose-dived beyond salvation and had to be abandoned as losses. "It's blackjack, Arnold," was the most common explanation.

If I looked at the history of this fiasco, and I subtracted our stupid expenses, and if I assumed that all the augmented wins counted at full value (as most of our losses were at full negative value), and if I removed the hours booked by spotters who never placed a bet, we were probably within one standard deviation of our expectation, a negative deviation, but nothing all that unusual. Some players were net winners, some were losers, but there was no single player who had booked enough hours for his personal result to be outside the realm of statistical normalcy. Yet, there we sat, after eighteen months, with 2,000 hours of play, and half our original bank.

Teams are great fun when you're winning, but can be hell when you're losing. Blackjack is always blackjack. The risk is always there!

♠ ♣ ♥ ♦

15

Shuffle Tracking

Years ago, when all mutiple-deck shuffles were fast and simple, numerous card counters independently discovered the most accessible form of shuffle tracking — *slug location*. You're sitting in a shoe game, watching the count climb ever upwards, and just when it reaches what must be an all-time high, the cut card emerges. As your spirits sink, you stare at the undealt cards — the *cutoffs* — which must contain nearly every paint and faint in the shoe. You continue to stare at that glorious slug of high cards, even as the dealer slaps it on top of the discards to begin his shuffle routine.

To your joy and amazement, when the dealer finishes shuffling and hands you the cut card, *you're still staring at that slug!* True, it's somewhat dispersed, but most of it's right there in the bottom third of the six-deck stack of cards in front of you. You cut this segment to the top of the pack and the cards soon verify exactly what your eyes had seen. For the next two decks, tens and aces just pour out of that shoe. For blackjack players, this is how shuffle tracking was born. It was a purely visual thing. It had nothing to do with voodoo, guesswork, or advanced mathematics. It was a logical extension of card counting.

In the early 1980s, prior to the outlawing of concealed blackjack computers, the most sophisticated computers were the shuffle-tracking computers. Shuffle-tracking was not difficult for a computer. Keith Taft, who had pioneered with the first perfect strategy computers, developed numerous successful shuffle-tracking computers. When the casinos learned of these devices, they took strong countermeasures. Thus were born the multi-pass, multi-pile, multi-slug shuffles that predominate to this day. When blackjack computers were outlawed, in the mid-1980s, the computers disappeared but the weird shuffles remained. Legends still circulated within the casino industry about the blackjack wizards who could track shuffles without computer assistance.

Although I was not a high-stakes player, I was one of those supposed wizards. I had learned shuffle-tracking theory through numerous discussions with various computer tracking experts, and had developed various crude methods for mentally tracking shuffles. It was much more difficult to track shuffles in addition to card counting, but I enjoyed the mental challenge. Over a period of ten years, I came to prefer tracking to straight card counting, despite the growing complexity of the shuffles.

Then, in 1994, Shuffle Master announced that they would be introducing their new 6 and 8-deck shoe shuffler, which would totally eliminate the possibility of shuffle tracking. It seemed the days were numbered for my favorite method of play, and most card counters had never even learned the strategies. My most guarded secrets had never been revealed, and now it appeared the opportunities to exploit the shuffles would soon be gone.

So, in September 1994, I published Part I of my three-part series on shuffle tracking in *Blackjack Forum,* urging counters to hurry and grab the profits that remained, as I assumed the end was near. Technology would soon eliminate the human shuffles.

This was the single most popular issue in the 14 year history of *Blackjack Forum.* Printed in an edition of 2,500 copies, I had to reprint another 1,000 within 8 weeks. Gamblers Book Club in Las Vegas, which had a standing order for 200 copies, called within a month to order another 100. According to GBC, it was not the players who were buying up the issues, but the casino personnel! Pit bosses, shift managers, surveillance officers!

I thought doom was just around the corner. But, unbeknownst to me, the reason the casinos wanted to learn to track shuffles was because they hated the new automatic shuffling shoes. It was one more expensive contraption that dealers disliked, and players mistrusted. It jammed frequently, required maintenance agreements, leases and paperwork ad nauseam. The casinos wanted to learn to track shuffles so that they could recognize trackers and they wouldn't need the blasted machines!

A funny thing happened. A lot of surveillance and pit personnel discovered that shuffle tracking was not an easy trick, but an advanced card counting strategy that required far more discipline than traditional counting. The ironic result is that the industry has taken an about-face on the whole issue. The time-consuming multi-pass shuffles are being replaced by the quick and dirty, old-style, one-pass, riffle-and-restack shuffles that make tracking easier!

When I wrote the *Blackjack Forum* shuffle-tracking series in 1994, I knew of only two one-pass, riffle-and-restack (R&R) shuffles in the state of Nevada. None in Atlantic City. A few in Canada. None elsewhere.

As I write this in November of 1997, there are one-pass R&R shuffles at a dozen different casinos in Las Vegas, including many major Strip properties. There are one-pass R & Rs now being used as house shuffles in both Reno and Atlantic City, and at dozens of casinos throughout the Midwest, the South, and the Western states. On the Blackjack Forum Web Site, we constantly update this information in our restricted, players-only Greenbelt area. I expect this trend to continue. Despite a handful of skillful trackers, the casinos simply make much more money by dealing out so many more hands per hour to the public.

Serious players may want to study the *Blackjack Forum* shuffle-tracking series, which is still available, for more advanced information on shuffle tracking. But if you're struggling now just to keep the running count, don't even dream about shuffle tracking. If you can't visually estimate deck segments in a discard tray, you will not be able to track segments.

I believe that most capable card counters, who play primarily in shoe games, should be employing some of the simpler tracking techniques. So, this is a crash course in the simplest tracking methods I know. If you are new to card counting, don't even try to learn any of these techniques at this time. Until you are a competent and experienced counter using traditional methods, this chapter will probably just confuse you.

You cannot track shuffles unless you open your eyes, observe, and think. You must learn to identify the weak points in a shuffle. I can provide you with the tools, but you have to learn to use them. This much I guarantee to the truly dedicated: the next time you go into a casino, you will look for profitable games in a whole new way. The number of decks, the rules, the penetration — *all take a back seat to the shuffle.*

TERMINOLOGY

In describing shuffles and shuffle actions, it is necessary to use a consistent terminology. You should always begin describing a shuffle, as you would any blackjack game for a card counter, with the number of decks and average penetration (shuffle point). From the segment tracker's perspective, this information tells you the approximate size of the *discards* and the *cutoffs*. A six-deck game with 75 percent penetration is viewed by a segment tracker as 4½ decks of *discards* and 1½ decks of *cutoffs*.

Riffling is the common dealer action of interleaving two *grabs*. A *grab* is that portion of cards which a dealer picks up in one hand. *For a segment tracker, the number of riffles the dealer performs is irrelevant.*

Stripping is an action in which the dealer holds a grab in one hand while pulling cards from the top and dropping them onto the table. Stripping makes no difference to a segment tracker, so we will ignore it. When we say that two segments are riffled together, they may in fact be riffled and stripped numerous times; it doesn't matter; we simply need to know that they are *married.*

A riffle of half deck grabs will produce a one-deck *stack.* An initial *stack* of all the cards in the shoe will always be *broken* into *piles* prior to shuffling. Today many casinos *break* the initial *stack* into 4 or more *piles.* Dealers take their *grabs* from these *piles* in order to *restack* their shuffled cards.

There are two basic types of multi-deck shuffle routines: the *riffle-and-restack* and the *stepladder*.

A *riffle-and-restack* (R&R) action means that the dealer will build a *final stack* by placing his riffled grabs one on top of another. In the traditional R & R routine, once two grabs have been shuffled together, they are not re-riffled with any other grab.

A *stepladder* action begins like a normal R&R action. The dealer riffles grabs from pile A and pile B to begin building a separate final stack. But instead of just placing consecutively riffled grabs from A and B on top of one another, as in the traditional R&R, the dealer starts taking one of his grabs from the *final stack* he is building, and marrying it with grabs from *alternating piles.*

A *one-pass* stepladder describes a shuffle which is completed when the piles are gone, and the final stack is offered for a player to cut. A *two-pass* stepladder is a shuffle where the final stack is rebroken into piles for a *second stepladder action.* Stepladders are time-consuming, so multi-pass stepladders are rare. Multi-pass R & R's are more common. More common still is a combination of a stepladder followed by an R&R (or a *combo*).

All R&R's and stepladders can be performed from two or more piles. You might find a 4-pile stepladder comboed with a 2-pile R&R. All shuffles which have more than two piles utilize a *criss-cross* pattern of grabs. A fairly standard criss-cross shuffle uses 4 piles in a square, with the first alternating stepladder grabs drawing an x-pattern, hence the name. I will use the term *criss-cross,* however, to define any shuffle in which there are *more than two piles,* and in which the cards from one pile will be mixed with cards from *more than one other pile.*

A *segment* is any visually identifiable portion of a stack or a pile. For example, you might refer to the bottom 1-deck *segment* of the discards. A *slug* is another word for a segment, though *slug* usually refers to a segment which has been identified as containing a large portion of either high cards or low cards.

In defining a shuffle, it is always important to note where the *cutoffs* are placed in the discards. They may be *topped, bottomed* or *plugged. Plugging* the cutoffs is *inserting* them into the midst of the discards. *Multiple-plugging* is breaking the cutoffs into two or more pieces, and inserting these pieces into different locations within the discards.

LET'S MAP A SHUFFLE

To start with, you have to study a shuffle *and learn it.* You must be able to reproduce the house shuffle on your kitchen table. You do not need the finesse of a professional dealer in the riffling and stripping actions, but you must be able to do the complete routine, albeit in your own slow and sloppy fashion. Then you break it down *on paper* into its various actions. Until you break down a shuffle on paper, you cannot map it.

We're going to start with an old Nevada classic you won't find anymore, the 4-deck, 75 percent penetration, two-pile, one-pass R & R. Here's how we break it down on paper:

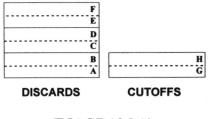

(DIAGRAM A)

Three decks are stacked in the discard holder. From the bottom, which is the order in which they entered the discard holder, these decks are identified in half-deck *segments* as Segment A, Segment B, and so on. One deck remains in the *cutoffs,* and this deck is also identified as half deck segments G and H.

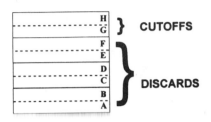

(DIAGRAM B)

The cutoffs have been *topped,* placed on top of the discards.

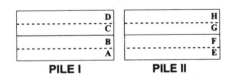

(DIAGRAM C)

The full stack has been broken into two 2-deck *piles.* The top half of the stack is now on the table on the right side of the bottom half. We identify these piles as Pile I and Pile II.

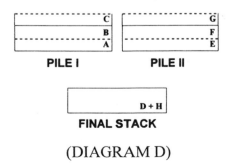

(DIAGRAM D)

A half-deck grab has been taken from the top of each pile. These grabs have been shuffled together, then set on the table to begin building the *final stack*. Note that in the final stack we have erased the dotted line which divides the half-deck segments. Since segments D and H have been married, we have no separate information on the distinct halves of this deck.

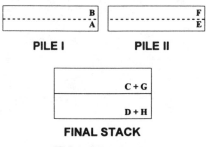

PILE I   PILE II

| C + G |
| D + H |

FINAL STACK

(DIAGRAM E)

The dealer has now married the next two half-deck grabs, placing them on top of the final stack he is building.

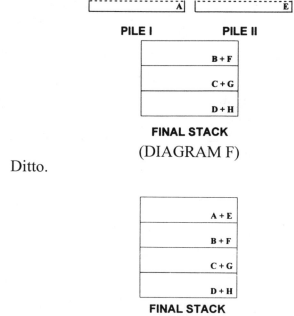

PILE I   PILE II

| B + F |
| C + G |
| D + H |

FINAL STACK

(DIAGRAM F)

Ditto.

| A + E |
| B + F |
| C + G |
| D + H |

FINAL STACK

(DIAGRAM G)

The shuffling process is complete.

THE MAP

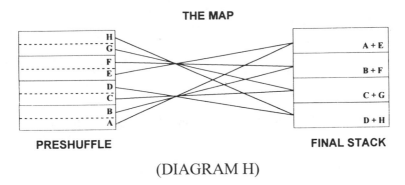

PRESHUFFLE   FINAL STACK

(DIAGRAM H)

The map (Diagram H) shows us clearly where every preshuffle segment is now located in the final stack. This means that if you had kept a separate running count on each of the preshuffle segments as they were placed in the discard holder, you would know the running count on each of the full-deck segments in the final stack. You may now choose to cut high cards to the top, or the low cards out of play.

A couple of fine points:

Let's say you are using the Hi-Lo count. Although you did not count the cutoffs, segments G and H, you can assume that the running count on the full cutoff deck will *balance* the total running count on the counted decks. I.e., if the total running count on the counted decks is -8, then the total running count on the cutoff deck is +8. For the purpose of marrying the segments, you would assume that segments G and H each had a running count of +4. (In fact, they will more likely not have such an even distribution, but you must use the best assumption.)

The accuracy of your map will depend on two major factors: your ability to visually identify segments by size and location, and the dealer's consistency in his grabs. Also, you will note that I broke down this shuffle with a one-deck cutoff portion. In fact, the cutoffs will be variously sized from shuffle to shuffle — *even when the dealer is consistent in his cut card placement,* as most dealers are. Depending on the number of players at the table, and the number of cards required to satisfy all hands after the cut card has come out, the actual cutoffs will vary in size from about ½-deck to 1 full deck (assuming the cut card is placed 3 decks deep). When the cutoffs are *topped,* as in this shuffle, a deeper deal provides more accurate distinct running count information on segments G and H.

In counting this game, the simplest method is to get a running count on half-deck segment A and retain it, then get a running count on half-deck segment B, and retain it. Then do the same for segments C and D. If you need to use some method of arranging chips, or your fingers, or your toes or whatever to remember these counts, then do what you must. When you get to segment E, you start *adding it to your count on segment A*, knowing that these segments will be married, and will comprise the top deck of the final stack.

Then you start adding the count of segment F to your stored count on segment B, etc., until you have a running count on each of the four decks in the final stack, from the top to the bottom.

Technically, assuming you are playing against a very consistent dealer, whose grabs are always equivalently sized, you don't even need to watch the shuffle!

Unfortunately, you are unlikely to find a shuffle quite this simple today. Let's map an actual 4-deck game that exists today. I know many casinos that use a variation of this shuffle. Variations in the number of decks in play, grab sizes, and even the number of piles, are minor variations that can be easily adjusted for with the breakdown and mapping procedure. I would describe this shuffle as a 4-deck, 75 percent penetration, one-pass R&R, 4-pile criss-cross, with half-deck grabs, and cutoffs double-plugged in the top and bottom halves of the discard pile.

The most important identifying factors to a segment tracker are the "one pass" and "R&R" designations. What deep penetration means to a card counter, *one-pass R&R* means to a segment tracker. One-pass R&Rs today are often complicated with cutoff plugging and multi-pile criss-cross grabs.

If you have four decks of cards, get them out and follow along as we break down and map this shuffle.

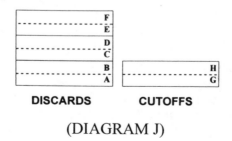

(DIAGRAM J)

Three decks have been dealt and placed in the discard holder. One deck is behind the cut card. As with our prior example, the actual size of this cutoff deck will *vary significantly* according to the number of players at the table and how many cards are required to satisfy those players' hands after the cut card comes out. The actual discard pile will, therefore, vary from 3 to 3½ decks in height, and the cutoffs will vary from ½ to 1 deck.

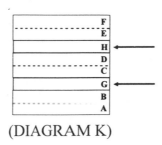

(DIAGRAM K)

The cutoffs are broken in two and *plugged* into the discards. For convenience, in the diagram, I have broken the one-deck stack of cutoffs into two half-deck segments, and plugged segment G precisely between bottom deck A/B and middle deck C/D. Segment H is plugged precisely between middle deck C/D and top deck E/F.

This actual house shuffle simply requires the dealer to break the cutoffs in two, and to plug one segment into the top half of the discards and the other segment into the bottom half of the discards. The top plug is generally inserted anywhere from half a deck down from the top, to the midpoint of the discards. The bottom plug is usually inserted anywhere from half a deck up from the bottom to the midpoint of the discards.

So, let's redraw the 4-deck preshuffle stack from scratch:

PRESHUFFLE

(DIAGRAM L)

I know it looks like I'm cheating, but bear with me. We've eliminated the plugs from Diagram K and restacked the decks (Diagram L) so that we can more easily describe the next actions:

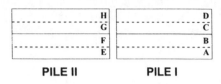

PILE II   **PILE I**

(DIAGRAM M)

The stack is broken into two 2-deck halves. Note that I've pulled the top two decks to the left side, or to the dealer's right, if you prefer. For the sake of consistency, I will always refer to left and right *as you look at the action*. The next break looks like this:

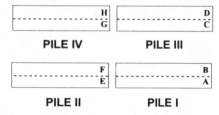

PILE IV   **PILE III**

PILE II   **PILE I**

(DIAGRAM N)

The dealer has broken each 2-deck pile into two 1-deck piles by taking the top deck from each 2-deck pile and placing them behind the first two piles. Next, the riffling begins:

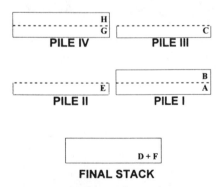

PILE IV   **PILE III**

PILE II   **PILE I**

D + F

FINAL STACK

(DIAGRAM O)

The first riffle routine is accomplished by riffling half-deck grabs from piles II and III.

Next, the classic criss-cross grabs are riffled:

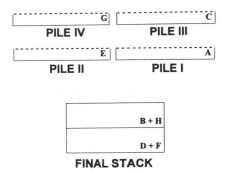

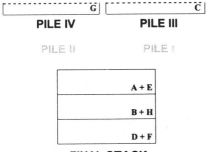

(DIAGRAM P)

The second riffle stacks half-deck segments B and H, from piles I and IV, on top of the first riffled deck.

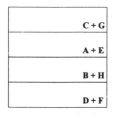

(DIAGRAM Q)

Piles I and II are eliminated as the half-deck segments A and E are riffled and stacked.

(DIAGRAM R)

The riffle and restack process is completed, and a player is offered the cut card.

Dealers only differed from each other in the placement of their pile breaks, with most making a first break to the left, and some making that first break to the right. If you do observe a dealer who uses a different sequence of grabs, resulting in either different marriages or a different sequence of marriages, you must do a separate breakdown for each variation.

This R & R shuffle employs various countermeasures designed to foil shuffle trackers. First of all, the cutoffs are broken into two pieces and *plugged* into the discards. This not only makes *cutoff tracking* problematic, but it *alters the discard stack.* A card counter who knows the count on each half-deck segment in the discard holder will lose this information when the cutoffs are plugged. Diagram R only looks promising until you recall that we *erased the plugs* we showed in Diagram K, and began Diagram L with redrawn decks.

Even if you found a dealer who always plugged the cutoffs into the same approximate areas of the discards — i.e., always one deck down from the top and one deck up from the bottom — there is no simple method for adjusting all of the individual deck counts in order to segment track the complete shuffle. This is because the size of the cutoff portion varies by as much as half a deck, depending on how many cards are required to be dealt following the appearance of the cut card, and as previously noted, the actual size of the discard pile also varies in size conversely.

All in all, this is a fairly lengthy and complex shuffle which has many built-in anti-tracking features. But one tracking process, called "tops and bottoms," is extremely simple and quite powerful against this type of shuffle. The tops and bottoms technique is also one of the easier tracking procedures for solo players. With a one-pass R & R, it is powerful against any dealer.

Let's start with the *bottoms.* What if I told you that the first half-deck segment of cards that went into the discard holder during play, i.e., segment A (the *bottoms*), would *always* end up in the second deck from the top of the final stack when the dealer offers the cut? The position of the bottoms, as per the above map, is true regardless of whether the dealer initially breaks the four-deck stack to the left or to the right. Nor does it matter what size the cutoff portion is, nor where in the discards the plugs are inserted, *so long as no plug is inserted directly into these bottoms.*

How do we know where the bottoms will end up? By comparing our preshuffle stack (Diagram L), with our final stack (Diagram R), and removing all information which may have been contaminated during the plugging process. This is a true map of what we actually know, despite the plugging. So long as no plug contaminates the bottoms, you can easily map them.

THE TOPS & BOTTOMS MAP

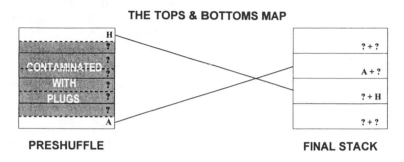

PRESHUFFLE   FINAL STACK

(DIAGRAM S)

Note that most of the information in this map is useless because of the "random" cutoff plugging that contaminated the middle of the shoe. The top half deck, however, and the bottom half deck, were not contaminated, so for the tops and bottoms, the map is accurate.

Any time a casino plugs the discards, look to the tops and bottoms for tracking possibilities. To clarify this for yourself, get out four decks of cards stacked one on top of the other, but turn the bottom half deck face up. Now, go through the complete shuffle routine we just defined. If you want to plug the cutoffs, do it; just don't plug into that bottom half deck. When you finish the complete shuffle routine, note where the face-up cards (the bottoms) are located. Now do it again, but this time break to the right instead of to the left. Note that the bottoms still end up in that second deck from the top. Now experiment with the tops.

This hands-on mapping technique is very useful when you are analyzing complicated shuffles. It will also give you a good idea of what happens when the dealer's grab is too large or too small, as your own grabs will likely be less than perfect. I recommend that you always test your map with actual cards after you have completed the breakdown on paper. Trackers who fail to do this often fail.

For a good card counter, bottom tracking in a one-pass R & R is fairly easy. All you do in this particular game is get the running count on that bottom half-deck as it enters the discard holder. If you remember nothing more for the rest of the deal, if you totally ignore the dealer throughout the shuffle procedure, you will know when the cut card is offered that those bottoms are located one deck down from the top. (Assuming that the dealer *uses* the house shuffle. I am *not* advising you not to watch!)

If the bottoms have a minus count (which means they are heavy in tens and aces), you can cut them to the top, or just play with this knowledge if some other player gets the cut. Likewise, if the bottoms were heavy in low cards (high plus count), you can bet small in this segment, or (if possible), cut it out of play.

Tracking the *tops* is similar to tracking the bottoms. First, our map (Diagram S) shows us that the top half deck in the discards (Segment H) — *which is also assumed not to be broken by plugs* — will always end up in the deck directly beneath the bottoms (if the dealer breaks the four-deck stack to the left, as in my example). If the dealer breaks to the right, however, the tops will end up in the *bottom deck* of the final stack!

As a practice exercise, do a shuffle break down and map on paper, using this same shuffle, but breaking the initial post-plug, four-deck stack to the right instead of to the left. Prove to yourself that the tops in this case will end up in the bottom deck. Now do it with cards, using a face-up top slug. See for yourself!

It is a bit more difficult to get a running count on the tops because you don't know exactly how many cards are going to end up in the discard holder. But based on the number of players at the table and the cut card placement and appearance, you should have little trouble estimating this count with a bit of practice.

The tops are more likely than the bottoms to be contaminated by a sloppy dealer break. A dealer may break a pile unevenly, then adjust for this by pulling cards from a tall pile onto a short pile in order to level off the piles. If you are playing versus a dealer who frequently does this, find another dealer.

Once you get proficient at top and bottom tracking, you will find that you can often track slugs other than the tops and bottoms. If this is a game in which you are able to play frequently, it would be to your advantage to memorize where all eight half-deck grabs are located pre- and post-shuffle. In fact, I would recommend all beginners in this type of game to only track the tops and bottoms. You will find many profitable opportunities even if you stick to the easy stuff.

In our tops and bottoms map, we disregarded 75 percent of the segment information because of plug contamination. If we assume the plugging process to be random, and we assume that any portion of the discards other than the tops and bottoms are liable to be contaminated, *and we really don't know where those plugs went,* then this is a valid conclusion. The fact is: *you have eyes.* From shoe to shoe, and dealer to dealer, the plug locations may be more or less random, but on any given shoe, the plugging happens before your eyes!

When you see a rich vein of money cards go into the discard holder, are you going to write it off as useless information just because it *might be* contaminated with a plug later? Should you perhaps keep your eyes on that slug while the plugging is taking place? Maybe it won't be contaminated at all but just raised to a new segment location. Maybe just the top or bottom of that slug will get shaved by a plug. Maybe the cutoffs themselves will be rich, and a plug will lengthen and enrich that slug! As long as your eyes are open, the plugging process is *not random.* For a good segment tracker, plugging the cutoffs, in any number of multiples, is just a minor bother. Visually following slugs is a talent that builds with practice. Visual identification of what is happening during the shuffle *must be practiced.*

THE POST PLUG MAP

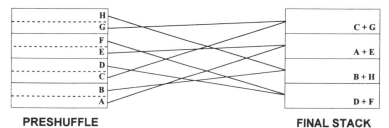

PRESHUFFLE   **FINAL STACK**

(DIAGRAM T)

Also, study your post plug map for other useful slug location information. I found numerous dealers at this casino (most, in fact) who always plugged the cutoffs into the same approximate locations. Dealers are creatures of habit. Some dealers always plugged *at least* a full deck down from the top and up from the bottom of the discards. These dealers provided me with twice as much reliable segment information.

For instance, if you look at Diagram T, which is a map of all of the post plug segments after the cutoff plugging had been done and the deck segments redrawn in Diagram L, you will note that all of the discarded *bottom* deck (A/B) is located in the consecutively stacked middle two decks. You'll also note that the *tops*

(Segment H) are combined with the top half of the bottom deck (Segment B). Such a dealer thus allows the slug locator to get the count on a *full deck segment* which is not contaminated with any other untracked cards! This is extremely powerful information to get shoe after shoe, as you may play from the very top to the very bottom of this segment. When both segments that comprise this deck are rich, as will happen on occasion, you will be in shuffle trackers' heaven! (Try not to rip the cut card out of some poor civilian's hand, or worse, try not to strangle the jerk when he cuts this segment out of play!)

Although I've described a very specific shuffle routine, note that these methods will work very well with any one-pass R & R. Depending on the number of decks in play, the penetration, the placement or plugging of the cutoffs, the number of piles, the riffling pattern and grab sizes, your map will change. The postshuffle locations of the pre-shuffle segments will be different. But with any one-pass R & R, slug location is fairly straightforward and extremely powerful.

Multiple piles and criss-cross riffling patterns simply confuse amateurs. I've found that multiple pile routines are *easier to track* than traditional two-pile routines. Since many experienced dealers make consistently clean breaks, this makes the shuffle truer to your map, and less affected by individual dealer quirks.

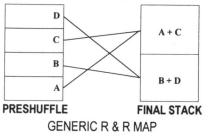

PRESHUFFLE   FINAL STACK

GENERIC R & R MAP

(DIAGRAM U)

Diagram U shows the generic map for all two-pile R&R shuffles, which is true regardless of the number of decks in play or the dealer grab sizes. The properties of the standard two-pile riffle-and restack shuffle insure that:

a) The top of the pre-shuffle stack will go to the bottom of the final stack;

b)The bottom of the pre-shuffle stack will go to the top of the final stack;

c)The upper portion of the bottom half of the pre-shuffle stack will go to the bottom of the final stack; and,

d)The lower portion of the top half of the pre-shuffle stack will go to the top.

What this means is that whenever you find a two-pile R&R, one of the easiest tracking techniques is to just play the *best half* of the shoe. This is extremely easy to do in practice.

For instance, in an 8-deck game, the player would obtain a running count on the first two decks placed into the discard tray, ignore the next two decks, then add the running count of the 5th and 6th decks placed into the discard tray to the running count of the first two decks. This combined running count will be the running count on the top 4-deck half of the final stack.

Assuming a balanced count is in use, we can assume that the bottom 4-deck half of the final stack will have the same running count but with the opposite +/- sign.

For many years, when the two-pile, one-pass R&R was the standard shoe shuffle used by most casinos, many trackers used this *best half* method of tracking regardless of the number of decks or dealer grab sizes.

Two-pile, one-pass R&Rs are no longer common, but this property of two-pile R&Rs which identifies the *best half* of the shoe is often useful in two-pass shuffles, as the most common second pass *is* a two-pile R&R.

This is a very important point because it identifies the type of information you're seeking to obtain by the end of the first pass. Many big money players often prefer to use tracking methods which simply identify the best half of a shoe, as opposed to more exacting methods which identify one or more relatively small, but very strong, slugs. Playing the best half allows for a less radical betting strategy. To flat bet your big bet through 4 decks of an 8-deck shoe, regardless of what the count does (and it should be *going down*), knowing that you have an average advantage of ½ percent to one percent throughout this half of the shoe, is near perfect camouflage.

All of these properties of two-pile R & R shuffles are just as true in multi-pile criss-cross R & R shuffles, the only difference being that the preshuffle segments have been rearranged.

PRESHUFFLE	POST R & R	POST STEPLADDER
H		
G		
F		$1/64$ **D + H**
E		$1/32$ **D + H**
D		$1/16$ **D + H**
C		$1/8$ **D + H**
B		$1/4$ **D + H**
A	**D + H**	$1/2$ **D + H**

FINAL STACK LOCATIONS OF FIRST TWO GRABS

(DIAGRAM V)

THE STEPLADDER

With a *stepladder* shuffle, the dealer begins by breaking the pre-shuffle stack into two or more piles. He begins building his final stack by marrying a grab from each of two piles, just as he would with a standard R&R shuffle. After he has married these first two grabs, however, all subsequent marriages include one grab from the final stack and one from another (alternating) pile.

The stepladder shuffle was developed specifically as an anti-tracking countermeasure. It dilutes the length and the strength of any individual marriages in the final stack. Compare the final stack locations of two preshuffle segments after a 2-pile stepladder routine to the final stack locations of the same two preshuffle segments after a 2-pile R&R. We'll assume a 4-deck game with $1/2$-deck grabs, and we'll map segments D and H (the first two grabs) only. (See Diagram V.)

We can see here that the stepladder action does, in fact, dilute the marriage of grabs D and H. Still, this is not in any sense a thorough dilution. Note that the bottom deck of the stepladder retains 75 percent of the initial marriage. This is important. For tracking purposes, you may assume that when the dealer uses a stepladder action, *75 percent of any grab remains in the final stack segment where it was initially married in.* Naturally, you must watch the shuffle actions to visually verify the dealer grab

161

FINAL STACK LOCATIONS OF SECOND TWO GRABS

Preshuffle stack (top to bottom): H, G, F, E, D, C, B, A

Post R & R: C + G

Post Stepladder (top to bottom): $1/64$ G; $1/64$ C + $1/32$ G; $1/32$ C + $1/16$ G; $1/16$ C + $1/8$ G; $1/8$ C + $1/4$ G; $1/4$ C + $1/2$ G; $1/2$ C

PRESHUFFLE   POST R & R   POST STEPLADDER

(DIAGRAM W)

sizes, adjusting the final stack location(s) of slugs according to what your eyes tell you, in conjunction with your map.

If segments D and H formed a marriage in the R & R shuffle which contained eight excess high cards in that bottom deck of the final stack, then we assume that the bottom deck of the stepladder final stack had only six excess high cards (75 percent).

Now compare the post-shuffle locations of segments C and G (the next two grabs) after both an R&R and a stepladder. In Diagram W, we see that in the R&R shuffle, grabs C and G are introduced into the final stack *at the same time* so they are located in the same final stack segment, one deck up from the bottom. In the stepladder shuffle, however, C is married into the final stack *a half-deck earlier than G*, so the major strength of C is located a half-deck below the introduction of G.

Also note that with a stepladder action, all of the dilution occurs *upwards*. Since grab G is first married into the final stack one deck up from the bottom, *it does not dilute downwards* into the bottom deck. This is a very important point to remember about stepladder shuffle actions. This upward dilution means that later grabs will all be located in the upper half of the final stack, and that the final grabs, A and E, will all be located in the top deck and a half.

So, although the stepladder does dilute the marriages, it is anything but a thorough dilution. The final stack locations of strong slugs remains very predictable, with slugs retaining about 75 percent of their initial strength.

In mapping stepladders, it is most practical to ignore the weak information, and retain only the strong. The most practical way to map the final stack of a stepladder is by showing each segment's major and minor strength. Graphically, we can do this by using upper and lower case letters to indicate major and minor strength based on where each grab was initially married in:

E + a
A + f
F + b
B + g
G + c
C + (d + h)
D + H

(DIAGRAM X)

Again, we'll assume a 4-deck game with half-deck grabs, but keep in mind that these principles carry over to any number of decks, and to all grab sizes. Multi-pile criss-cross shuffles merely change the order of the segments in the final stack.

Note in Diagram X that virtually all of segment E in the final stack of the stepladder is located in the top deck, and that segment A is all located within the top deck and a half. The segments which become the dealer's last grabs will always provide the strongest information you will obtain on a stepladder shuffle.

Note that the bottom half-deck of the final stack of the stepladder is entirely made up of cards from the first two grabs, D and H. Again, this is very strong information, especially if you can track both segments.

So, the stepladder is a dilution shuffle, but it is also very trackable and the major strength (75 percent) of identified slugs should remain in the final stack where they were initially married in. The two-pile stepladder shuffle also retains the basic property of the two-pile R&R, in that the top and bottom segments of the pre-shuffle stack reverse order in the final stack.

All of the methods for tracking and mapping multi-pile shuffles, and cutoff plugs apply to stepladders as well as to R&Rs. Many casino experts believe the stepladder is far more effective at slug dilution than it is. In fact, it is a highly predictable shuffle for slug locators.

To track the more complex shuffles in use today, a player must have a keen eye. Card counters should already have developed some of the visual skills needed to track shuffles. Those who use true count systems should already be adept at estimating the penetration according to the height of the stack of cards in the discard tray. Shuffle trackers must refine this talent.

As with card counting, practice definitely will increase your visual skills. You should use the visual drills described below both to advance your abilities as well as to gauge your talent.

Most players look at any shuffle almost as a form of sleight-of-hand magic. *Now you see it, now you don't!* The fact is that the cards enter the discard tray right in front of your eyes. They are never removed from your sight. The dealer uses no legerdemain to confuse you when he mixes the cards. He is merely following the required house shuffling routine. Don't be intimidated by complex shuffles.

How Much Can You See?

The major skill required for shuffle tracking is *eyeballing* — the ability to quickly visually estimate the sizes and positions of identified slugs, dealer break points in relationship to these slugs, plug placement, and dealer grab sizes. As with card counting, some players will discover they have a natural aptitude for eyeballing. Most of us must practice this skill to develop it.

With 8 decks of cards and two felt tip marking pens, one black and one red, you can make yourself a set of *slug readers.* Use standard casino cards which are in good condition. Here's how to do it:

1. Remove all jokers.

2. From 6 of the 8 decks, separate out all of the tens, jacks, queens, kings and aces.

3. Using the black marker, color the lengthwise edges of these high cards (tens and aces) on *one side only.* This can be done very quickly and precisely if you hold the cards in a tight pack (50-60 cards at a time) while coloring one edge. You want this edge to appear as *solid black.*

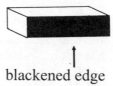

blackened edge

When you shuffle these marked cards back into the remaining unmarked cards, you will be able to read the high card slugs with 100% precision! Be careful when you shuffle *not to spin* any cards 180 degrees, which would result in some of the blackened edges being on one side of the pack and some on the other side. You want a 6-deck stack of cards which you can read when the blackened edges are turned towards you, but which appears to be normal when the blackened edges are turned away.

Now, take the remaining two decks and use the red tip marker to color one lengthwise edge of *all* of these cards. Set these two decks aside, as they will be used later for more advanced practice techniques.

Start your practice with a 4-deck pack of cards. Unless you have worked as a dealer with multiple decks, 6-deck packs are fairly unwieldy for the average person. You would likely find it convenient to have a discard tray for stacking the cards.

Shuffle the cards using whatever method is easiest for you, but shuffle thoroughly. The purpose of this exercise is simply to practice *eyeballing,* not tracking, so any home style shuffle will do if it mixes the cards. After shuffling the cards, turn the reader edges towards you. You are looking at the precise distribution of the money cards in the full stack.

There are two common types of high card distribution in a stack — *bar codes* and *shading.*

bar codes <
shading <
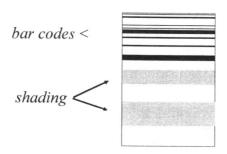

Bar codes are caused by solid runs of high cards, and are usually short in length. Isolated bar codes — unless they are particularly thick — are not worth much to a segment tracker. What you are looking for are multiple bar codes concentrated in proximity to each other.

Shading is caused by an excess of high cards which are not bunched together in solid runs, but spread through a segment of cards. The heavier the distribution of high cards, the darker the shade. The bigger a shaded segment is, the more valuable it is.

Ask yourself: *If I could see this edge while playing, where would I make my big bets?*

Now, turn the pack of cards around so that you cannot read the slugs, and use a joker to cut just one good betting opportunity to the top. With the joker still jogged out from the side edge, turn the reader edge towards you. Did you hit your mark? If not, remove the joker and do it again. Do it until you hit it.

Shuffle the cards and repeat this exercise. You will probably get pretty good at this in a short amount of time. When you find that you are always able to hit your cut point within a few cards, it's time to increase the degree of difficulty.

Shuffle the cards and visually identify the *best two slugs* in the stack. Now turn the reader edge away from you and use two jokers to cut to the tops of both slugs. This exercise will teach you to visually read the slugs in the discards.

In a casino you won't ever have that blackened reader edge to show you the pattern. But, as you see slugs enter the discard tray, you must mentally burn that pattern on to the edges of the cards, just as you did at home when you studied the blackened reader edge, then turned it away from you.

Once you are proficient at identifying slugs in full 4-deck and 6-deck stacks of cards, you're ready to increase the degree of difficulty again. Shuffle the cards, study the reader edge, then turn the reader edge away from you, then break the stack into two piles. Then locate the slugs using the jokers.

After you get good with a 2-pile break, breaking the way a dealer would in a casino, practice breaking to both the right and the left, and breaking to both the outside and the inside. Learning to follow multiple slugs through the breaks is not easy for most players. Expect to spend many hours and many days at this exercise if you want to increase your level of skill at this.

Each time you increase the degree of difficulty, it's best to start the new exercise with the identification of just one or two of the biggest slugs. If you try to do too much at once, you'll just frustrate yourself. This is a good exercise to practice with a friend. It's more challenging and closer to real world casino conditions if someone else breaks the stack into piles. Also, be sloppy with your breaks. Don't try to avoid cutting slugs in two, and don't attempt to make perfectly even piles.

Bear in mind that there is nothing magical nor mystical about eyeballing. You're just training your eyes to recognize and follow invisible patterns. After you get proficient at following slug patterns through breaks, you're ready to start using the two decks with the reddened edges to mimic *plugging the cutoffs.*

Shuffle. Study the reader edge. Note the slug positions. Turn the reader edge away from you. Take a plug from the reddened pack, and insert it into the stack *with the reddened edge facing away from you.* After you straighten the stack, use jokers to mark the slugs *as well as the plug.* Turn the stack around and check your work.

After you become proficient at eyeballing with a single plug, using various sized plugs, move on to double plugs, then triple plugs. Finally, when you can accurately identify the significant high card slugs through multiple plugs *and multiple pile breaks,* you are on your way to being the player the casinos fear most — the player who has the visual talent to track virtually *any* human shuffle. I am assuming, of course, that your card counting skills are already top notch and that you understand and use the basic tracking skill of *mapping shuffles* prior to attacking them.

If you do not grasp the theories of tracking, eyeballing talent will be useless. The theories, however, are fairly straightforward and logical. Most card counters have no problem grasping tracking logic when that logic is presented. The difficult part is utilizing the methods of tracking in a casino.

You do not need to be a total whiz at multiple slug and plug eyeballing in order to beat most shuffles. What is important is that you recognize your skill level, and that you only bet your big money according to what *you know,* based on *your skill.* As your eyeballing skills increase, more complex shuffles become profitably attackable, and beatable shuffles become more beatable.

You will discover in the casino that it is not really that difficult to burn the edges of the discards mentally with the slug patterns, because the discard tray fills relatively slowly, allowing you all the time in the world to watch those patterns take shape. In fact, as soon as I see a slug worth tracking, I immediately start considering which segment(s) of the discards it might be married to, according to the map for the shuffle being used.

In choosing games, be smart — always go for the shuffles that are most trackable according to *your skills*. Look for the simplest, one-pass, R&R shuffles, if any are available. Look for casinos that *top* the cutoffs, instead of plugging them, and that use fewer plugs. The simpler the shuffle, the easier it will be to track. The more complicated shuffles become accessible as your visual skills build. Shuffle tracking has the potential for making shoe games more profitable for card counters than one-deckers.

MULTI-PASS SHUFFLES

There are dozens of different shuffle actions in use today, most developed in the past ten years to combat trackers. Do not be intimidated by a shuffle action you have not seen before. Try it at home with a marked slug and see what it does. Many actions have no dilution effect; they just rearrange segments.

Multi-pass shuffles are now more common than single-pass shuffles, though this trend appears to be reversing. If multi-pass shuffles are the only types of shuffles that are available where you play, then you must take your time in attempting to track them. You must map each pass separately on paper, and it would also be wise to use some of the excellent and inexpensive software on the market for mapping shuffles.

Multiple passes dilute the slugs, as well as the advantages which occur, but they are often excellent for identifying the best half or best third of the shoe. If you can follow your slug from the discards through the first pass, then you can follow it again from the first through the second pass. The process remains the same.

ESTIMATING YOUR ADVANTAGE

I advise using a quick and dirty method for estimating your advantage at the tables. Let's say I've cut the one-deck segment which contains the bottoms to the top of the shoe. Let's also say I had a Hi-Lo running count of -10 on the bottoms. If I'm fairly certain that *all* of the ten excess high cards are now located in the top deck, based on my having visually verified that the dealer's grab on the bottoms assured this, then I would quickly estimate my true edge to be about 5 percent off the top of this deck.

First, however, I must adjust this advantage downward to account for the fact that I know that the ½-deck segment of cards which was married to the bottoms came from 3½ decks that were *shy* ten high cards. Any individual ½-deck segment would, therefore, be expected to be shy by about 1½ high cards. Therefore, I'd actually only expect to see 8½ excess high cards in this segment. I would conservatively round this down to 8. A very simple conservative rule in this game would be to deduct one count for every five, so that 10 becomes 10 - 2 = 8.

It is also best to further knock down this estimated true edge due to the *inevitable* less-than-perfect grabs. If the dealer shaved a few cards off my slug, or added a few, and/or if the grab he married it to was slightly larger than my slug, this would further reduce my estimated true edge. (In fact, the unknown segment, or cards added or subtracted to my slug, may actually increase the value, but since I do not know their value, I *must* assume that they will reduce the value, as this is more probable.) Based on my visual eveidence, if I truly felt my full slug was retained, and that the segment it was married to was not noticeably larger, etc., I would likely decrease my estimate of a running count of 8 to a running count of 7. When tracking, it is always better to err on the conservative side. If I was not so sure of the full slug retention, etc., I might knock the estimated running count down to 6, 5, or even 4. It's better to be safe than sorry.

Traditional card counters hate this type of imprecision. What started out as a count of 10, has now become something between 4 and 7, based on my *feel* for it. Unfortunately, if your insistence on precision keeps you from making these types of conservative estimates, you will regret it. Some trackers, just to be on the safe side, simply cut every slug value in half for betting and playing purposes. If you find its easier to be consistent in this way, instead of going by your feel for your visual estimates, then just call 10 high cards 5 and be done with it. *This is much safer than calling it 10 or 8!*

But, let's say I settle on an estimated running count of 7 for this one-deck segment. This would be a true edge of 3½ percent. Now, I deduct the house edge off the top, say ½ percent, and I would assume that my true advantage off the top is an even 3 percent. If I am using the Hi-Lo Lite, I will not only bet accordingly, but play my hands accordingly. Since the Hi-Lo Lite makes strategy adjustments at true edges of 0, +2, +4, +6, etc., I will play the +2 strategy right off the top. The Lite approach to strategy indices makes it easy to know how to play within your slugs. The blocks of changes are widely spaced so that you have little room for uncertainty. With any estimate of from 4 to 7 extra high cards in a one-deck segment, I will be playing the +2 true edge strategy. With 8 to 11 excess high cards, I play the +4 strategy.

Note, and this is important: I will commit to playing this strategy *throughout the entire one-deck segment.* I will start my running count at 0, as always, but I will remember that it is always estimated at +7 higher as it goes up and down through the segment. However, if my running count goes down to -8 on the first round, I will *not* assume that my true edge of 3 percent has disappeared. It is, in fact, far more likely that the unknown segment that was married to my segment also contained excess high cards than it is that all of the excess high cards in my segment clumped into the first round of play.

As you go through the segment, you may slowly cut back on your bet if many excess high cards, over and above what your slug contained, continue to come out. And perhaps on the last round of the segment, cut back to a small bet. But the easy rule to remember is to just bet and play that sucker from top to bottom like you've got a 3 percent edge! Believe me, you will play your slugs far more accurately, and make lots more money with this approach, than if you drop your bet as soon as your "estimated" running count goes back down to 0.

It is more profitable, and accurate, to *estimate your edge conservatively,* but then to *play the slug with aggression.* If you are getting your slugs, and you will know when you are because you will see the paint on the felt, *get your money on the table.*

What if the high cards don't come out on the first round? What if you bet multiple big money hands, and a bunch of garbage hits the table? If I am fairly certain that I caught my slug, I would deduce that this round is due to bad cards in the unknown segment, and I will continue to bet it up. I may even raise my bets. If I am unsure, then I will pull back. I will also be kicking myself, because if I am unsure, I should not have been betting it up in the first place. Tracking is not a guesswork strategy. But note: often you will not be playing slugs so rich in high cards that it is impossible for these cards not to paint the table on every round. You will play many slugs that have just 3 or 4 estimated excess high cards. Even if you are tracking accurately, you will not see paint every round.

If the slug you identify is a low card slug which you are cutting *out of play*, and if you have no other useable slug information, use the same method of advantage estimation *in reverse*. If I cut out a one-deck slug with 10 excess low cards identified in half of it, I'll assume 10 - 2 = 8 low cards have been removed from the remaining 3 decks. Depending on how accurate I feel about the dealer's grabs, etc., I may knock this down to 6, 5, or 4 low cards removed. If I settle on 6, I will estimate my true edge as 6 / (3 x 2) = 1 percent. After subtracting the house edge off the top, I'll estimate my advantage at about ½ percent.

Note, incidentally, how much more valuable it is to cut a +10 slug to the top than it is to cut a -10 slug out of play. For this reason, you should usually give precedence to cutting a high card slug to the top, as opposed to cutting a low card slug out of play, if you have to decide between the two actions.

Coming off the top of a shoe with big bets is the most profitable method of play for a segment tracker. It is also the best camouflage a card counter can use in casino blackjack, as most casinos believe their tracking countermeasures are effective. (And they are! Most counters simply cannot do this!)

Do not waste a lot of mental energy attempting to estimate your precise advantage at the tables. You are simply looking for a slug that provides a high enough expected count to justify your big bets. When you locate it, go for it. Whether you estimate your precise advantage as 3 percent or 4 percent is immaterial. Always bet conservatively, never more than 2-3% of your bankroll, even with an estimated advantage of 6-10%. Such rich situations will occur, but as long as you bet conservatively, you will avoid disaster. Dealer sloppiness, unknown segment information, and your personal errors must always be factored in.

SHUFFLE-TRACKING TEAMS

Segment trackers will find many unique opportunities for team play. One of the most powerful methods of play is a variation on the BP/spotter approach, where the spotter is a tracker who calls the BP in *at the top of the shoe,* after the slug of high cards has been cut to the front. This is one of the most deceptive, impossible to identify, attacks that can be made.

Two-person tracking teams, with one good tracker and one capable card counter, will often find it advantageous to play at the same table. Multiple simultaneous hands are more advantageous for slug trackers than for traditional card counters.

If you're playing on a $100,000 bankroll, and you estimate your advantage on a slug to be five percent, a half-Kelly bet would allow a single-hand of $2,500. If your low bet is generally $25, with a spread from $25 to two hands of $500 each, you don't want to raise suspicions by suddenly betting into the thousands. With two players, you can spread to four or five hands of $500 each, and get substantially more money on the table, while also cutting your risk from half-Kelly to about quarter-Kelly.

Multiple-hand play is also more advantageous for trackers because you will be betting into known, limited areas of the shoe, often with other players at the table. If you are playing in a slug that will last for one deck, then disappear, you want as much of that slug for yourself as you can get. If there are three other players at the table, and you play a single hand, then each round will consume, on average, 13 cards. So, this slug will last four rounds, and you will get four hands. If you play four simultaneous hands, each round will consume about 19 cards. In two rounds, you will get eight hands, and there will still be 14 cards left in the slug. Even if the casino allows bets of multiple thousands, it is less risky to spread this money to multiple hands, and it looks better.

With two players at the table, you will also double your likelihood of getting the cut card. If one player is female, you can often *be assured* of getting the cut card. Many blackjack players like to "let the girl cut," particularly if she's asking to do it.

It is easy to signal the cut point to a non-tracker. The tracker knows where the slug is located in the pre-riffled piles, as he has visually, but nonchalantly, followed the plugging/breaking process. He pays *no attention* to the shuffle, except out of the corner of his eye. When the dealer grabs his slug, he give an inconspicuous signal — i.e., places his right hand on the rail, or touches his wedding ring. The non-tracker knows that the dealer is now riffling the slug. When that segment gets slapped onto the final stack, the cut point is right at the top. As the dealer stacks segments on top of it, the edges of each riffled segment remain visible as offset lines on the final stack. When the dealer finally squares up the full stack, removing those segment lines, the cutter must note the approximate cut point one last time, as accurately as possible, then nail it.

♠ ♣ ♥ ♦

16

SPECIAL RULES

Some casinos offer rules which can be beaten, but not with traditional card counting strategies. We'll look at a few of the more popular of these rules. Generally speaking, if you see a new rule or option on a blackjack table, it is probably not beneficial, and almost assuredly would not be beneficial if you are guessing at the value and the proper strategy. Casinos often introduce options in order to seduce players into making bad decisions. All of the options described in this chapter were introduced for that purpose, but some have proven to have some value to smart players.

OVER/UNDER

One of the more popular options (unfortunately not popular enough!) is *over/under.* This is an optional side bet (actually two separate bets) you may make that your first two cards will total either over 13 or under 13. Their is a special area on the table layout for you to make these bets. Ace always counts as 1 for this bet. A total of 13 always loses. If you win, you are paid 2 to 1.

This rule is most often offered on 6 and 8-deck games. It has little value with a traditional card counting system. Using the Hi-Lo Lite, you would need a true edge of +2½ to just to break even on the over bet, or -3 on the under. These advantages will not occur very often, unless the penetration is quite deep.

A better counting system for this option is to count the ten-valued cards as -1 and Aces, 2s, 3s, and 4s as +1. Using this counting system, you would make an over bet at a true edge of +1½ or greater, and an under bet at -2 or lower. This greatly increases the value of the options. If you know the Hi-Lo Lite indices, you may use these strategy changes with the over/under count for strategy plays on your blackjack hand. In a 6-deck game, with 75 percent penetration, you could get close to a one percent advantage by using a 1-to-4 spread with proper over/under bets. With deeper penetration, the value skyrockets.

In some European casinos, there is an over/under variation in which a pair of aces pays a 7-to-1 bonus on under bets. This payout almost doubles the value of the over/under option. Unfortunately, there are very few over/under games anymore, and the casinos know that card counters attack them.

By the way, do not place over/under bets without using a card counting system. The house advantage is 6½ percent on over, and more than 10 percent on under, if you're just guessing.

ROYAL MATCH

This is a side bet offered in some single-deck games that you will be dealt two cards of the same suit. If so, you will be paid 3-to-1; if you are dealt a king and queen of the same suit, you will be paid 10-to-1.

Ironically, a card counter developed a system for beating this rule a few years ago, which he sold privately for a few months, then took it off the market. I examined the system, and also had the theory tested via computer simulation, and it worked!

Unfortunately, it was not very easy. You had to keep four separate counts (of the cards remaining in each suit), which did not appeal to many players. Do not bet on this option unless you are using a valid suit-counting system, however, as the house edge is 3.8 percent.

DOUBLE EXPOSURE

This is a variation of blackjack in which both of the dealer's first two cards are exposed. Sounds great, but there are some bad rules that go along with it. Blackjacks only pay even money, but worse than that, the dealer wins ties (except for blackjacks). This means that if the dealer has 20 and you have 20, you have to hit (and pray for an ace!).

Most double exposure games have poor rules, as these are primarily gimmick games for tourists. Card counters can beat these games. However, the strategy is quite complex. I personally do not believe there are enough double exposure games of value to make it worthwhile to study the strategy. Should you find a decent double exposure game somewhere, you will find

Stanford Wong's Hi-Lo Count strategy for beating double exposure in his *Professional Blackjack*.

SUPER SEVENS

This is a side bet invented by the same man who invented over/under, Ken Perrie. Essentially, you are placing a bet that you will be dealt one, two, or three sevens, with various payouts depending on whether they are suited or unsuited.

Technically, card counters can beat this option if they learn to keep a count of the sevens vs. the non-sevens. The perfect counting system for this option is to count all sevens as -12, and all non-sevens as +1. I no longer remember the true count at which it becomes optimal to place a Super Sevens bet, but it does occur occasionally.

The problem is that the option is not worth more than a few cents per hour to a seven-counter, due to that $1 maximum bet restriction. And since the counting system has virtually no value whatsoever to your regular blackjack hand, no one would ever waste their time learning it. Without the seven-count, the house has about a ten percent advantage over you on this bet, so it has no value to anyone.

Why did I figure out the counting system in the first place? Oh, yes, now I remember. Someone paid me to.

APPENDIX

Basic Strategy
For any Number of Decks

	2	3	4	5	6	7	8	9	X	A
STAND										
17	S	S	S	S	S	S	S	S	S	S
16	S	S	S	S	S	H	H	H	H[1]	H
15	S	S	S	S	S	H	H	H	H	H
14	S	S	S	S	S	H	H	H	H	H
13	S	S	S	S	S	H	H	H	H	H
12	H	H	S	S	S	H	H	H	H	H
A7	S	S	S	S	S	S	S	H	H	S[2]
DOUBLE DOWN										
11	D	D	D	D	D	D	D	D	D[3]	D[4]
10	D	D	D	D	D	D	D	D		
9	D	D	D	D	D					
8				D	D					
A8					D[5]					
A7		D	D	D	D					
A6	D[5]	D	D	D	D					
A5			D	D	D					
A4			D	D	D					
A3			D	D[5]	D					
A2			D	D[5]	D					
SURRENDER (LATE)										
17										¢[6]
16								¢[7]	¢	¢[8]
8-8										¢[9]
15									¢[10]	¢[7]
7-7									¢[5]	¢[9]

S = Stand   H = Hit   D = Double Down   ¢ = Surrender

1 = Stand with 3 or More Cards
2 = Hit in 1-Deck, or if Dealer Hit Soft 17
3 = European No-Hole Hit
4 = Multi-Deck or European No-Hole Hit
5 = Single-Deck Only
6 = Hit Soft 17 Only
7 = Single Deck Hit
8 = Single Deck, X-6 Only
9 = With Hit Soft 17 in Multi-Deck
10 = Excluding 8,7

Pair Splits

	2	3	4	5	6	7	8	9	X	A
	No double after splits									
AA	$	$	$	$	$	$	$	$	$	$[1]
99	$	$	$	$	$		$	$		
88	$	$	$	$	$	$	$	$	$[1]	$[1]
77	$	$	$	$	$	$				
66	$[2]	$	$	$	$					
33			$	$	$	$	$			
22		$[2]	$	$	$	$				
	With double after splits									
AA	$	$	$	$	$	$	$	$	$	$[1]
99	$	$	$	$	$		$	$		
88	$	$	$	$	$	$	$	$	$[1]	$[1]
77	$	$	$	$	$	$	$[2]			
66	$	$	$	$	$	$[2]				
44		$[2]	$	$	$					
33	$	$	$	$	$	$	$[2]			
22	$	$	$	$	$	$				

INSURANCE: NO

Surrender (early)

	2	3	4	5	6	7	8	9	X	A
17										¢
16								¢	¢	¢
8-8									¢	¢
15									¢	¢
14									¢	¢
7-7									¢	¢
13										¢
12										¢
7										¢
6										¢
5										¢

$ = Split   ¢ = Surrender

1 = European No-Hole Hit   2 = Single Deck Only

Hi-Lo Lite Strategy
For any Number of Decks

	2	3	4	5	6	7	8	9	X	A
STAND										
17	S	S	S	S	S	S	S	S	S	-2
16	-4	S	S	S	S	4	4	2	0	4/2
15	-2	-4	-4	-4	S	H	6	4	2	6/2
14	-2	-2	-2	-4	-4	H	H	H	H	8/4
13	0	0	-2	-2	-2/-4	H	H	H	H	H
12	2	0	0	0	0/-2	H	H	H	H	H
A7	S	S	S	S	S	S	S	H	H	0/H
DOUBLE DOWN										
11	D	D	D	D	D	D	-2	-2	-2	0
10	-4	D	D	D	D	-2	-2	0	2	2
9	0	0	0	-2	-2	2	4			
8	6	4	2	2	0					
7			6	4	4					
A9	6	4	4	2	2					
A8	4	2	2	0	0					
A7	0	0	-2	-4	-6					
A6	0	-2	-4	-4	D					
A5	8	2	-2	-2	D					
A4			0	-2	-4					
A3			0	0	-2					
A2			2	0	0					
SURRENDER (LATE)										
16						6	2	0	0	0/-2
8-8								4	0	
15						6	4	2	0	0
14							6	4	2	4/2
7-7									2	
13								8	4	

S = Stand H = Hit D = Double

Note: Table entries with slashes "/"indicate different decision numbers for Stand Soft 17 and Hit Soft 17, in format S/H. 4/2 Means the index is 4 if Dealer Stands on Soft 17, or 2 if the dealer Hits Soft 17.

HI-LO PAIR SPLITS

NO DOUBLE AFTER SPLITS

	2	3	4	5	6	7	8	9	X	A
AA	$	$	$	$	$	$	$	$	$	-2
XX		4	4	2	2					
99	0	0	-2	-2	-2	4	$			2
88	$	$	$	$	$	$	$	$	4[1]	$/0
77	$	$	$	$	$	$				
66	2	0	-2	-2	$					
33	4	2	0	0	$/-2	$				
22	4	2	0	$	$	$				

WITH DOUBLE AFTER SPLITS

	2	3	4	5	6	7	8	9	X	A
AA	$	$	$	$	$	$	$	$	$	-2
XX		4	4	2	2					
99	0	-2	-2	$	$	2	$	$		2/0
88	$	$	$	$	$	$	$	$	4[1]	$/0
77	$	$	$	$	$	$	2[2]			
66	$	$	$	$	$	$[3]				
44		4	0	0	-2					
33	0	-2	$	$	$	$	2[2]			
22	0	-2	$	$	$	$	2			

INSURANCE: 2 (1 in single-deck)

SURRENDER (EARLY)

	2	3	4	5	6	7	8	9	X	A
17									4	¢
16							2	0	-2	¢
8-8								4	0	¢
15							4	0	0	¢
14							6	4	0	¢
7-7							6	2	0	¢
13									2	¢
12									4	-4
7										-4
6									6	-2
5									6	0

$ = Split   ¢ = Surrender

1 = Split if below this index; 2 = One-deck always split; 3 = One-deck only

ZEN COUNT STRATEGY
FOR ANY NUMBER OF DECKS

	2	3	4	5	6	7	8	9	X	A
STAND										
17	S	S	S	S	S	S	S	S	S	-3/-2
16	-4	S	S	S	S	5	4	2	0	3/1
15	-2	-3	-4	-4	S	H	5	4	1	4/2
14	-1	-2	-2	-3	-3/-4	H	H	H	3	5/3
13	0	-1	-1	-2	-2/-3	H	H	H	H	H
12	1	1	0	-1	0/-1	H	H	H	H	H
A7	S	S	S	S	S	S	S	H	H	2/H
DOUBLE DOWN										
11	D	D	D	D	D	-4	-3	-2	-2	0
10	-4	-4	D	D	D	-3	-2	-1	1	1
9	0	0	-1	-2	-3	2	4			
8	5	4	3	2	1					
7			5	5	5					
A9	4	3	3	2	2					
A8	3	2	1	0	0					
A7	0	-1	-2	-3	-3/-4					
A6	0	-1	-2	-4	D					
A5	5	1	-1	-3	D					
A4		2	0	-2	-4					
A3		3	1	-1	-2/-3					
A2		3	1	0	-1					
SURRENDER (LATE)										
16						5	2	0	-2	-1/-3
8-8								4	0	
15						5	3	1	0	1/0
14							4	2	1	2/1
7-7									1	
13								5	3	

S = Stand   H = Hit   D = Double

Note: Table entries with slashes "/"indicate different decision numbers for Stand Soft 17 and Hit Soft 17, in format S/H. 2/1 Means the index is 2 if Dealer Stands on Soft 17, or 1 if the dealer Hits Soft 17.

ZEN PAIR SPLITS

	2	3	4	5	6	7	8	9	X	A
NO DOUBLE AFTER SPLITS										
AA	$	$	$	$	$	$	$	$	$	-2
XX	4	4	3	2	2					
99	-1	-1	-2	-2	-2	3	$			2
88	$	$	$	$	$	$	$	$	2[1]	$/0
77	$	$	$	$	$	$				
66	1	0	-1	-2	$					
33	3	1	0	-2	$	3[1]				
22	3	1	-1	$	$	$				

	2	3	4	5	6	7	8	9	X	A
WITH DOUBLE AFTER SPLITS										
AA	$	$	$	$	$	$	$	$	$	-2
XX	4	3	3	2	2					
99	-1	-2	-2	$	$	1	$	$		1
88	$	$	$	$	$	$	$	$	4[1]	$
77	$	$	$	$	$	$	1[2]			
66	-1	-2	$	$	$	$[3]				
44		3	1	0	-1					
33	-2	$	$	$	$	$	2[2]			
22	-2	-2	$	$	$	$	3			

INSURANCE: 1

SURRENDER (EARLY)

	8	9	X	A
17			3	¢
16	3	0	-3	¢
8-8		4	-1	¢
15	4	1	-1	¢
14	5	3	0	¢
7-7	5	2	0	¢
13			2	¢
12			5	-3
7				-3
6			6	-2
5			6	0

$ = Split   ¢ = Surrender

1 = Split if below this index; 2 = One-deck always split; 3 = One-deck only

Recommended Source Materials

These are the books on blackjack I really like, in alphabetical order by author. Some of the older ones are out of print, but most can still be located in used book stores. There are twenty-nine books on the list. If you read all of these, you will know a lot about blackjack. The ones that are marked with an asterisk (*) are the ones that are most relevant for modern day players. I've only marked seven of them this way. In my opinion, these are the really important books that any serious player should read. The books that are marked with two asterisks (**) are not so timely, but are classics that I learned a lot from. The books that are not marked at all are still books that I like a lot. I have many books on blackjack that did not make this list. These are all the good ones. I have purposely left all of my own books off this list.   — A.S.

**Andersen, Ian. *Turning the Tables on Las Vegas.* New York: The Vanguard Press, 1976.

Baldwin, Roger, Wilbert E. Cantey, Herbert Maisel, and James McDermott. *Playing Blackjack to Win.* New York: M. Barrons and company, 1957.

*Carlson, Bryce. *Blackjack for Blood.* Santa Monica: CompuStar Press, 1992; revised, 1994.

Chambliss, Carlson R. and Thomas C. Roginsky. *Fundamentals of Blackjack.* Las Vegas: GBC, 1990.

*Dalton, Michael. *Blackjack: A Professional Reference.* Merritt Island, FL: Spur of the Moment Publishing, 1991; third edition, 1993.

**Forte, Steve. *Read the Dealer.* Oakland: RGE Publishing, 1986.

*Griffin, Peter A. *The Theory of Blackjack.* Las Vegas: GBC, 1979; fifth edition, Las Vegas: Huntington Press, 1995.

Humble, Lance and Carl Cooper. *The World's Greatest Blackjack Book.* New York: Doubleday, 1980.

Malmuth, Mason. *Blackjack Essays.* Las Vegas: Two Plus Two, 1987.

Marks, Dustin D. *Cheating at Blackjack.* San Diego: Index Publishing, 1994.

Marks, Dustin D. *Cheating at Blackjack Squared.* San Diego: Index Publishing, 1996.

Noir, Jacques. *Casino Holiday*. Berkeley: Oxford Street Press, 1968.

*Perry, Stuart. *Las Vegas Blackjack Diary*. New York: Self-published, 1995; third edition, Pittsburgh: ConJelCo, 1997.

**Revere, Lawrence. *Playing Blackjack as a Business*. Secaucus, NJ: Lyle Stuart, 1969; last revised, 1980.

*Schlesinger, Don. *Blackjack Attack*. Oakland: RGE Publishing, 1997.

**Thorp, Edward O. *Beat the Dealer*. New York: Random House, 1962; revised edition, New York: Vintage Books, 1966.

Uston, Ken. *Ken Uston on Blackjack*. Secaucus, NJ: Lyle Stuart, 1986.

**Uston, Ken. *Million Dollar Blackjack*. Hollywood: SRS Enterprises, 1981.

**Uston, Ken. *The Big Player*. New York: Holt, Rinehart and Winston, 1977.

Uston, Ken. *Two Books on Blackjack*. Wheaton, MD: The Uston Institute of Blackjack, 1979.

Vancura, Olaf and Ken Fuchs. *Knock-Out Blackjack*. Las Vegas: Huntington Press, 1996.

**Wilson, Allan. *The Casino Gambler's Guide*. New York: Harper & Row, 1965-70.

*Wong, Stanford. *Basic Blackjack*. La Jolla: Pi Yee Press, 1992; revised 1993.

**Wong, Stanford. *Blackjack in Asia*. La Jolla: Pi Yee Press, 1979.

Wong, Stanford. *Blackjack Secrets*. La Jolla: Pi Yee Press, 19

*Wong, Stanford. *Professional Blackjack*. La Jolla: Pi Yee Press, 1975; last revised 1994.

Wong, Stanford. *Tournament Blackjack*. La Jolla: Pi Yee Press, 1987.

**Wong, Stanford. *Winning Without Counting*. La Jolla: Pi Yee Press, 1978-80.

Zender, Bill. *Card Counting for the Casino Executive*. Las Vegas: Self-published, 1990.

INDEX